Religion and *Life Issues*

GCSE Religious Studies for **AQA B**

Revision Guide

Lesley Parry, Jan Hayes
and Kim Hands

HODDER
EDUCATION
AN HACHETTE UK COMPANY

The Publishers would like to thank the following for permission to reproduce copyright material:

Photo credits

Cover © Don Hammond/Design Pics/Corbis; **p41**, *tl* © Flip Schulke/CORBIS, *tr* © Dinodia Images/Alamy, *br* © SCANPHOTO/PA photos. All other photos © Lesley Parry.

Although every effort has been made to ensure that website addresses are correct at time of going to press, Hodder Education cannot be held responsible for the content of any website mentioned in this book. It is sometimes possible to find a relocated web page by typing in the address of the home page for a website in the URL window of your browser.

Hachette UK's policy is to use papers that are natural, renewable and recyclable products and made from wood grown in sustainable forests. The logging and manufacturing processes are expected to conform to the environmental regulations of the country of origin.

Orders: please contact Bookpoint Ltd, 130 Milton Park, Abingdon, Oxon OX14 4SB. Telephone: +44 (0)1235 827720. Fax: +44 (0)1235 400454. Lines are open 9.00–5.00, Monday to Saturday, with a 24-hour message answering service. Visit our website at www.hoddereducation.co.uk.

© Lesley Parry, Jan Hayes and Kim Hands 2010
First published in 2010 by
Hodder Education,
An Hachette UK company
338 Euston Road
London NW1 3BH

Impression number	5 4
Year	2014 2013 2012

Illustrations by Oxford Illustrators, Richard Duszczak and Gray Publishing
Typeset in Minion 11/13pt by Gray Publishing, Tunbridge Wells
Printed in India

A catalogue record for this title is available from the British Library.

ISBN 978 1 444 11240 5

Contents

Using this guide to revise

REVISION – It's that horrible word we all don't like hearing! It is used by teachers a lot but what do they actually want you to do? Revision is a means to an end. It is a process of learning to enable us to sit an exam and pass it. But how do we do it? Is there a right way or wrong way?

I hate revision

Well we can assure you, as the three writers of this guide, we asked the same questions at all levels of our education (and yes, revision was something none of us liked either); we all teach students currently; we are all experienced in writing and marking exam papers, and we want you to pass your exams and give yourselves the best options in your future. The hate, the 'not wanting to do it' might never go away but it is our aim to pass to you some ways of doing it which will enable you to achieve your best in RS and your other exams. You might find that when you get 'how to revise', you actually enjoy the process more, and get more out of it. We know the feeling of being faced with books and files full of two years' work that we have to remember across many subjects; everyone telling us our futures depend on this work – and at 16 there are so many other things that we could be doing which are far more enjoyable!

How are we supposed to learn all this?

Simple fact is it has to be done – however you do it. So how does this guide help?

- As a starter, each topic starts with an overview and key terms page, which very simply tells you what the topic is, and what words you NEED to learn (because they could be asked about in the exam).
- Then each topic goes on to tell you the basics of what you need to revise for each topic – there are at least four pages on each topic of the key ideas to tackle the key questions that come up in the exam. *Learn them.* There is also a page of teachings to use with the topic – it is an RS exam after all!

- Each topic also gives you a revision technique – how to revise. *Try them all out* and use the ones you felt most comfortable with.

They tell us to revise but I don't know how!

- Each topic gives you some sample questions. *Practise and check your readiness for the exam* by doing these. These have some sample answers which are commented on so you can see the good and bad characteristics in them. *Build your technique by incorporating the good and cutting out the bad.*
- These are followed by an actual sample full question – have a go, then look at someone else's effort and see if you can improve it. These have comments to help see what they are worth.
- A thought map is given for each topic – it provides the basics, but the fine detail needs to be supplied by you.
- Finally, each topic gives you a checklist, so you can work out how best to approach each topic, and where you need to focus your energy. *Use it before you begin revision – to work out what you need to do most on – and after – to double check you know it all.* All in all, it is giving you the information and the tools to do well in the exam.

Well guys I think we can answer these issues in a variety of ways

Our aim is to start to narrow down WHAT you need to know, give you tips on HOW to learn it, think about the TYPE of exam questions you could be asked and most importantly give you the CONFIDENCE to know you have prepared well.

GOOD LUCK!

Religious teachings that can be used in all topics

For each religion you study, there are several key beliefs and teachings, which you can use to support your answers to questions about the attitudes of religions to any topic. Learn these for the religion(s) you have studied.

Many of these can be applied to a variety of topics so learning **one** teaching can be used again and again – which means **less learning**!

> **Tip**
>
> Highlight a teaching and list the topics it can be used in – makes learning easy.

Buddhism

- Karma – our words/actions shape our future rebirths. We need to make sure these are positive.
- Each of the actions of the Eightfold Path.
- The Five Precepts (guidelines for living): ahimsa (not harming others), not clouding our minds, using kind language, not taking what is not freely given, no sexual misconduct.
- Compassion (loving kindness).

Sikhism

- Values of sharing, tithing, duty, tolerance, chastity, humility.
- The Khalsa vows – meditation and service to God, no use of intoxicants, no eating meat that has been ritually killed, equality of all, fight injustice, do not to hurt others.

Christianity

- Jesus said love God, love your neighbour.
- God created us all equal as he made us all.
- Justice – everyone is equal so we all deserve fairness.
- Forgiveness, love, compassion.
- The Ten Commandments.

Judaism

- Ten Commandments:
  - love only G-d
  - make no idols of G-d
  - do not take G-d's name in vain
  - keep the Sabbath holy
  - respect your parents
  - do not kill
  - do not steal
  - do not commit adultery
  - do not tell lies
  - do not be jealous of what others have.
- Equality, love, respect.

Islam

- Ummah – brotherhood of all Muslims means all Muslims are equal and deserve respect.
- All Muslims have to follow the Five Pillars so are equal in their duties to Allah.
- Shari'ah law (law originating from the Qur'an and Hadith) applied to modern life.

Hinduism

- Hindu virtues state:
  - ahimsa (non-violence)
  - compassion
  - honesty
  - respect for life
  - tolerance
  - service
  - self-discipline
  - support for others
  - wisdom.

Using quotations in answers for maximum mark impact

Every year, candidates lose marks because they don't make the best use of the quotes in their answers. If you want to get grade C or better, you need to use them effectively. Let's look at two examples.

Explain religious attitudes to the issue of abortion. *(6)*

Christians say do not kill in the Commandments. They think life is special because God made it. So they think abortion is wrong. Jews think the same as Christians. They say it breaks the commandments, and that life is special.

This candidate has mentioned teachings from two religions – they'd probably get three marks. To get more marks, they needed to spell out what the quotes meant in terms of abortion, like this:

Christians say do not kill in the Commandments. They think life is special because God made it. **They believe that life is there from conception, so having an abortion is killing and so breaking the commandment. Since there is a life, it is special, and an abortion is like saying it isn't.** So they think abortion is wrong.

The answer would be enough to get three marks for Christianity. If they did the same for Judaism – three more marks. If they had only studied one religion, they'd need to give more teachings, more application and more explanation. Probably to provide four different teachings, which are explained and applied, would get them to full marks.

Explain why some religious believers believe that violent protest is wrong. *(4)*

In the Bible it says 'do not kill'. It also says that life is sacred. Violence doesn't solve any problems either – it makes them worse.

This gives us three valid ideas, but does not answer the question – the examiner has to make sense of it in terms of protest. Sometimes, it isn't obvious enough, and the examiner gives no marks because to them it doesn't answer the question. If you do apply your quotes, you get more marks. A better answer would be:

In the Bible it says 'do not kill'. **Sometimes, violent protest is extreme, and can end up with people dying, like the animal rights protestors sending bombs to scientists.** It also says that life is sacred. **This includes those we disagree with, so violent protest is saying those people we fight aren't special, or their life isn't.** Violence doesn't solve any problems either – it makes them worse.

The second version does what it needs to – it explains its points. In the second answer did you notice that when quotes are applied, the ideas made are also developed so the answers are more detailed? This means higher marks.

Command words in the exam

Command words are the words that instruct you what to do in the exam. They help you to answer in the way the examiner wants, which gets you more marks. The command words you might encounter in the exam are explained below.

Make sure you learn these words and phrases so that you do what the examiner wants you to. This will guarantee you get better marks.

- Describe – give a detailed account of, as if you are painting a picture of something in words, same as 'outline'.

- Explain – when you make a point, expand it. If the question asks you to explain, and you just give a list of ideas, you will not be given more than half the available marks.

- Explain, using examples – expand the point(s) you make by giving examples of what you are talking about.

- Give – same as 'write down'; you can just give a list.

- How – same as 'in what ways', like 'how do religious people work for animal rights' is asking 'in what ways' they help animals.

- Name – is asking you for the actual technical word or name of something.

- Refer to – include in your answer. For example, you will often be asked to refer to religious beliefs and teachings, so you have to include some to get good marks.

- What is meant by – say what something means.

- Why – give reasons for something. For example, why do people choose to have children?

- Do you agree? Give reasons for your answer – you only get marks for saying why people agree and why they disagree, not for just saying they agree or disagree. You also need to give explanations to the points you make.

- … showing that you have thought about more than one point of view – you have to say why people agree and why people disagree.

- What do you think? Explain your opinion – this is asking you to give your own opinion on a statement, but the statement that is given always makes you think about religion.

How examiners mark your work: introducing AO1 and AO2

The exam has two types of questions: AO1 questions and AO2 questions.

AO1 (Assessment Objective 1) questions

These are questions that test your *knowledge and understanding* of the course details, and your ability to *apply ideas*. These questions are asking for explanations, descriptions and definitions usually. They also ask you for religious attitudes to things. Marks normally vary from one mark to six marks – the examiner has to ask two or three questions in total for this assessment objective in each full question, and together they have to add up to nine marks.

Some examples might be:

- What is meant by animal rights? (1)
- Explain what is meant by the term vegetarian. (2)
- Give **two** ways in which humans damage the environment. (2)
- Explain why some religious believers disagree with war. (3)
- Explain how religious believers help victims of prejudice. (4)
- Explain religious attitudes to abortion. Refer to beliefs and teachings in your answer. (5)
- Describe the problems young religious people can face in their lives. (6)

There are grids which an examiner uses to mark your answers to questions of three marks or above – let's take a look at a version of those.

Let's say your question is worth three marks – the examiner will use levels one to three of that grid. If it was worth six marks, the examiner might have to give you two lots of marks – one for each religion, each up to level three. They might have to allow for two marks within levels three and four, so level three could get you three or four marks, and level four could get you five or six marks – depending on the quality of your answer.

The point is that the same judgements are being made all through your paper and everyone else's to make sure it is consistent and fair.

Level mark	Descriptor	In plain English, that means …
Level 0 0 marks	Nothing relevant given	The answer is wrong, or irrelevant
Level 1 1 mark	Something relevant, which is worthy of a mark	Give just one simple idea – no explanations
Level 2 2 marks	Elementary knowledge and understanding	Give two ideas here. One idea explained would be fine
Level 3 3 marks	Sound knowledge and understanding	You need to give several reasons, and explain some of them. Or you could explain one idea in a lot of detail
Level 4 4 marks	A clear knowledge and understanding with some development/analysis	This is a clearly written answer, which flows. It gives ideas, but explains them in good detail as well

AO2 (Assessment Objective 2) questions

These are questions that test your ability to evaluate statements which are linked to the topic you have studied. It is really easy to spot these questions because they always start with a statement, and then ask what you think, or whether you agree. The 'What do you think?' questions are always worth three marks, and the 'Do you agree?' ones are always worth six marks. Here are some examples:

- **Religious people should not have abortions.** What do you think? Explain your opinion. (3)
- **Genetic modification of anything is playing God.** What do you think? Explain your opinion. (3)
- **Commitment ceremonies are the most important part of being religious.** What do you think? Explain your opinion. (3)
- **Peace is an impossible dream.** Do you agree? Give reasons for your answer showing you have thought about more than one point of view. Refer to religious arguments in your answer. (6)
- **Prejudice is the worst problem in the world today.** Do you agree? Give reasons for your answer showing you have thought about more than one point of view. Refer to religious arguments in your answer. (6)
- **All zoos should be closed down.** Do you agree? Give reasons for your answer showing you have thought about more than one point of view. Refer to religious arguments in your answer. (6)

You can see from the grid below that marking AO2 questions also takes into account the quality of your written English. Again there is a question and answers to help you see how it works.

Level mark	Descriptor	Quality of written communication	Tips
Level 0 0 marks	You give an unsupported opinion, or nothing relevant	Your work is almost impossible to understand	This answer is either restricted to 'I agree/disagree', or is blatantly not answering the question, or is impossible to read
Level 1 1 mark	Your opinion is supported by a simple reason	Your work can be read. The spelling, grammar, etc. isn't great, but we can understand what you mean	This is a very short answer, probably makes one point, or two points for two marks. Even if the English is terrible, as long as the examiner can read it you can get the mark
Level 2 2 marks	Your opinion is supported by two simple reasons (one or both sides)		
Level 3 3 marks	Opinion supported by one well-developed reason, or several reasons given across both sides. If there is no religious content, there is a level limit of three	Writing can be understood, and although there can be mistakes in spelling, grammar, etc., what is being said is still clear	So, your English can still have lots of mistakes in it to get this mark. It has to be clear, and make sense. Really you need to be writing in paragraphs – making points and explaining them to get four marks. Must *have* some religious stuff in here to get more than three marks
Level 4 4 marks	Opinion supported by two developed reasons. This can be on the same or different sides and must include religious content		
Level 5 5 marks	You have explored both sides of the argument through a series of points which are explained in good detail, and must include religious content	You write in flowing paragraphs with few mistakes in any aspect of your written English. You also use a lot of the proper words for things, e.g. the correct religious terms	You have to write coherently in terms of what you say – it makes good sense – as well as how you say it – good English. These aren't short answers, they are in paragraphs and show that the writer really knows what the question is getting at and how to challenge it
Level 6 6 marks	You have explored both sides of the argument through a series of well-explained points, and have applied your knowledge of religion very effectively to support your ideas		

Exam day – some tips

You've worked hard, revised well and along comes the day of the exam and you're sure it's all going to fall apart and you'll fail. On this page you'll find some tips and advice to cope with exam pressure.

Common sense

Let's start with the obvious: if you are feeling nervous on the day of the exam just remember the following few pointers:

- Most people will be feeling nervous, it's your adrenaline pumping you up.
- You have prepared well, so you are going to be able to answer the questions.
- Exams are written to be user friendly, the examiner wants you to do well.
- Remember you don't have to write a perfect paper to get a good grade – just do your best.

Exam day

- Start the day before – get a good night's sleep – teenagers need nine hours!
- Eat breakfast – sounds daft *but* your brain needs fuel!
- Don't try and revise in any depth now, but you could just glance over a couple of revision postcards or run through a few mnemonics to get your brain in gear.
- Arrive at the exam hall in good time, but not too early – a lot of waiting around is likely to make you more nervous – unless you have your memory cards to hand.
- Think positive – tell yourself you are going to do well because you are!

Coping in the exam

- Before the exam starts settle your nerves with some breathing and relaxation exercises.
- Focus your mind on your space rather than gazing around the room.
- Make sure you can see a clock – you need to be able to time how long you spend on each question.
- When permitted, read through the exam paper before you start answering questions, pick the paper up, actually handling the paper helps calm your nerves.
- Decide the order of the questions you are going to answer; many people find it helps to answer questions on their strongest topic areas first, it gives you confidence to deal with the ones you find more difficult.
- Take mini-breaks in the exam – when you finish a question pause for a few moments before starting the next question.
- If you panic in the exam, put your pen down and take a mini-break, sit back and take a few deep breaths before continuing.
- If your mind goes blank on a question – don't panic, leave space to write an answer and move on, you can come back to that question at the end.
- When you finish – go back over your paper question by question; check that you have done everything required.

> 'Venus told me that champions don't get nervous in tight situations, that helped me a lot. I decided I shouldn't get nervous, just do the best I can'
> (Serena Williams)

Topic One Religion and animal rights

Overview

For this topic, you need to know about:

- different ideas about the status of animals
- animal rights and protecting those rights
- the issue of animal extinction, and preservation of endangered species
- how we use and abuse animals in the modern world
- issues surrounding farming and slaughter of animals
- attitudes to diet.

For each of these you need to be able to explain specific terms, give examples to show your understanding, explain why people may agree or disagree with the issues, write about problems associated with them, and give religious attitudes to them.

You also need to be able to evaluate (agree with and disagree with) statements about these issues.

Definitions of key terms

You could be asked to define any of these in the exam, or the phrases could be used in questions.

Animal experimentation – experiments carried out using animals as the test subject, e.g. for testing cosmetic toxicity or for new drugs.

Animal rights – the rights animals have to live without cruelty, and to have good treatment.

Battery farming – farming where the animals are kept in small pens or cages and are prevented from roaming freely.

Bull-fighting – a sport in which trained matadors fight bulls, usually leading to the bull's death.

Cloning – producing an organism exactly identical to another asexually.

Companionship – living with, or keeping someone company, e.g. a pet cat.

Extinction – where a whole species has been wiped out, so that no more exist, and in the future cannot exist again.

Free-range farming – farming where the animals are allowed to roam in the open.

Fur trade – an industry which breeds animals to sell their fur in clothing, etc.

Genetic modification – where DNA is taken and adjusted or modified then reinserted into an egg, which is then placed into an animal's womb to produce a replica of the original.

Hunting – the practice of pursuing an animal with the intention to catch and kill it.

Ivory trade – illegal industry which sells items made from ivory, e.g. elephant tusks.

Preservation of species – actions taken to keep a species in existence, e.g. zoo breeding programmes for endangered animals.

Status of animals – the value animals have, which then decides their rights, e.g. are they as valuable as humans, or not?

Vegan diet – diet which does not include any meat, meat products or dairy products.

Vegetarian diet – diet which does not include meat or meat products.

Zoo – place where animals are kept for the general public to look at.

Topic basics 1 – The status of animals

A core area of this topic is the difference between humans and animals, and the status that gives each one. Clearly, humans think they are more important – just think how we treat animals and the rights we give them (or don't!). So what is the difference and why is it the belief?

Are humans and animals equal?

Yes
- All created by God.
- All live in the same world and depend on the same resources.
- Dependent on each other.
- Just different species of the same world.

No
- Humans are cleverer.
- God gave humans control over animals.
- Humans have a soul.
- Impact of humans is greater so not equal.
- We can kill animals, but cannot kill other humans.

How do humans and animals differ?

- Humans have greater impact on the world around them, e.g. building, clearing land, including potentially destroying it, etc.
- Humans use logic and reasoning to work things out, animals work from instinct.
- Humans have a soul.
- Humans follow moral codes; animals follow nature and instinct.
- Humans communicate in more complex ways, e.g. language.

Religions and animals

The symbols show which religion believes each point; where there is no religion stated it is true for all:

- God created animals then humans. ✝ ☪ ✡ ☬
- Humans are more important.
- Humans can use animals for their own benefit, e.g. eat, experiment, etc.
- Humans have responsibility to look after animals (God's creation).
- Animals are part of cycle of rebirth/ reincarnation, just like humans. ✸ ॐ
- Abusing animals has a consequence in our future life – either at Judgement Day, or in being reborn.

Animal rights: what do we mean?

Animal rights: the rights animals have to live without cruelty, and to have good treatment. This means we can't just do what we want with them or to them. They have the right to be treated properly, fairly and with kindness – even when we intend to kill them. Laws in the UK protect domestic (pet) animals, farm animals and endangered species. They do this by enforcing the looking after of animals – food, water, shelter, and no cruelty.

Practise your evaluative skills

Do you agree or disagree that it is wrong to …

- Use animals as food?
- Treat animals equally to humans?
- Use animals as experimental test subjects?
- Give animals rights?
- Believe humans have dominion (ownership and control) over animals?

Topic basics 2 – How humans use animals

Uses of animals: some examples

- As pets/companions – cats, dogs, birds, mice, hamsters, rats, guinea pigs.
- As exercise – horses.
- As workers – guide dogs, police dogs, customs dogs, hunting dogs, hunting birds; also as beasts of burden (pulling ploughs, carts, etc.).
- As providers – sheep (wool), cows (milk), hens (eggs), bees (honey).
- As food – lamb, cows, hens, deer, pigs, fish.
- As experimental test subjects – mice, rats, monkeys, dogs.
- As sport – bulls (bull-fighting), birds (shooting), deer/rabbits/hare/fox (hunting).

This isn't an exhaustive list – you will be able to think of many more. You don't need to though – there are more than enough examples for any exam question there. Think about this – which ones are good, which ones are bad? Why?

Animals as companions and helpers

This includes the pets we have, cats and dogs, for example. It also includes guide dogs for blind people, hearing dogs – animals which are both companions and helpers to people. Perhaps we can use the term 'friend'.

Key issues
- These animals bring great comfort to humans.
- These animals seem to have a higher status than others.
- These animals seem to have more rights than others because of that status.

Animals as workers for transport

Animals that work are sometimes called 'beasts of burden' because they can do a lot of heavy work as a team with humans. They might be used to transport loads, to plough fields and other farm-related tasks especially in developing countries. We also now use animals to find explosives and drugs and do a myriad of other work tasks.

Key issues
- Beasts of burden are often worked to death.
- These animals need special training, which can be harsh, or give them an élite status.
- This is not a natural life for them, and they can be poorly treated, although it can also give them a special status, e.g. police dogs.

Farming of animals

Nearly all the food we eat comes from farms: dairy products, crops and meat. These foods are crucial to our survival. Cheaper meat usually comes from factory farms using battery farming methods. Farms also produce free-range meat (animals allowed to roam free), which is more expensive.

Key issues
- Animals are just treated as products.
- Farming means they live unnatural lives, which can be in cruel conditions.
- Many animals are fattened and killed before they reach adulthood.

Animals in hunting

This is the chasing and killing of animals and birds. Hunting could be for food, fur or sport.

Key issues
- Traps used in hunting are cruel, often not killing an animal quickly, and catching unintended victims, e.g. pet dogs.
- Just killing an animal for sport is immoral in many people's eyes – religious or not.
- Hunting is making some species extinct.

Animals in sport

Animals are used in a variety of sports such as horse and dog racing and blood sports. Blood sports result in injury to the animals, e.g. hunting, hare coursing, dog fighting. All should be regulated within British law. Many people enjoy the thrill of these sports.

Key issues
- Animals which don't make the grade are often slaughtered.
- Most blood sports are very cruel to at least one of the animals.
- These sports do not let animals live their natural lives.

Bull-fighting

Bull-fighting is a national sport of Spain in which a matador uses set moves to fight a bull, and eventually kill it.

Key issues
- Cruel to the bulls.
- The bull dies in great pain over a long period.
- Treatment of fight injuries for 'winning' bulls is poor – many die.

Animal experiments

Animals are bred deliberately as an experimental subject. Experiments are to test toxicity (how poisonous something is), medicines and medical techniques. The experiments are for the good of humans.

Key issues
- Animals can suffer greatly in experiments.
- Many experiments seem unnecessary, e.g. to test yet another version of a product which has already been tested.
- Animals cannot in any way live natural lives.

Animals in zoos

Zoos are places which keep animals from all over the world for people to see, as entertainment and education. Many have breeding programmes which produce animals for other zoos or to put back in the wild.

Key issues
- Animals are rarely in their natural environment or climate.
- Animals have less space than they have in the wild.
- Many zoo animals display clear signs of boredom and distress.

Genetic modification of animals

Genetic modification involves taking the DNA from an embryo, changing it and putting it back to create a new species of animal, e.g. genetically modifying a pig so that its heart can be used in human organ transplants.

Key issues
- Many people believe it is morally wrong to do this to animals when we don't know the exact outcomes.
- It costs a lot of money which many people believe could be used more effectively otherwise, e.g. for medical treatment.
- Donor/host animals don't get to live natural lives.

Animals in the fur and ivory trades

These are trades which deal in the sale of fur or ivory (elephant tusks). Fur farms are battery farms, which farm as many animals in as small a space as possible to increase profit. The animals they farm for their fur are usually not from that climate, e.g. mink (a cold weather creature) being farmed in Korea (a hot country).

Key issues
- Humans don't need fur as a material in the modern world.
- Elephants are killed simply for their ivory, which is a small part of them.
- Fur farms are very cruel.

Topic basics 3 – Treatment of animals and diet

This course wants you to know about how we treat animals – and what should or shouldn't be acceptable. Treatment is also linked to how we use animals in our diet, as food, and the laws religions have to do with food.

Treatment of animals at home

- People generally look after pets really well – they are friends.
- There are many laws to protect domesticated animals in the UK.

Treatment of animals in the wild

- We put food out for birds, hedgehogs, etc.
- Many species are endangered now because of human lifestyles, e.g. certain birds.
- We ignore most of them, and treat some as vermin, e.g. foxes and rats.

Preventing the extinction of animals

Many animal species are on the verge of extinction (dying out). This is often because of what humans have done. Many zoos try to breed endangered species to try to prevent extinction. Laws to protect species also exist.

Key issues

- Losing any species is a big blow to the ecosystem.
- Any species we lose is lost to our children – they will inherit a depleted world.
- Moral (and spiritual) guidance is to protect life not destroy it (stewardship).

Why be vegetarian/vegan?

A vegetarian diet does not include meat products, while vegans eat neither meat nor dairy products.

- Medical problem.
- Don't like the taste.
- Disagree with farming methods or slaughter methods.
- Think it is morally wrong to eat meat.
- Religious rules.

Slaughter of animals

In religions such as Judaism and Islam, it is fine to eat (most) meat, but the animal has to have been ritually slaughtered. This means a prayer of thanks is said before the kill; then, the animal is killed by having its throat slit, so that its blood is released. There may be prayers after, and any blood drawn from the pieces of meat.
Other religions might not have a precise process, but would expect animals to be humanely killed.

Food rules

Some religions have rules about the food they can or cannot eat.

Buddhism

- Many Buddhists are vegetarian out of respect for the cycle of rebirth.

Christianity

- Many Christians eat no red meat on Fridays, because Jesus died on Friday. This shows respect for his sacrifice on that day.
- Many eat no meat at all during the period of Lent.

Hinduism

- Most Hindus are vegetarian out of respect for life.

Islam

- No pork.
- Only meat from an animal which has been ritually slaughtered (halal).

Sikhism

- No meat from an animal which has been ritually slaughtered.
- Many are vegetarian out of respect for God's creation.

Judaism

- No meat and milk together.
- No pork.
- Only meat from an animal that has been ritually slaughtered.
- No blood.
- Only fish with fins, backbone and scales.
- Only meat of an animal which has cloven hooves and chews the cud.

Religious teachings: good specific teachings to learn

Sikhism

- If you say there is God in every being, why kill a chicken? (Guru Granth Sahib).
- God's light is in every creature (Guru Granth Sahib).
- Many Sikhs are vegetarian out of respect for God's creation and the langar serves only vegetarian food.
- All food is pure as God has given it for our sustenance (Adi Granth).
- Guru Gobind Singh stated that he enjoyed hunting – so it's not forbidden.

Buddhism

- The First Precept is to not harm other sentient beings.
- Correct livelihood – no job that exploits animals.
- All living things fear being put to death – let no one kill or cause others to kill (Dhammapada).
- Bodhisattva vow: 'as long as sentient beings suffer, I will be around to help'.
- The Buddha gave up his life in many lifetimes to help animals.

Christianity

- God made the world and gave humans dominion over it.
- Animals are part of creation and deserve respect and protection (Assisi Declarations).
- Jesus said God cares about even the sparrows.
- The earth and everything in it is the Lord's (Genesis).
- 'Scientists must abandon laboratories and factories of death' (Pope John Paul II).

Judaism

- G-d made the world and all in it.
- A righteous man looks after his animals.
- Do not be cruel to animals (Naochide Laws).
- Animals must be respected as they are G-d's creation but human life is always more important.
- Do not work on the Sabbath – nor your animals (Torah).

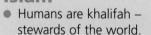
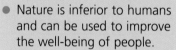

All religions teach: stewardship, sanctity of life and companionship

Islam

- Humans are khalifah – stewards of the world.
- Nature is inferior to humans and can be used to improve the well-being of people.
- Showing kindness to an animal is an act rewarded by Allah.
- Muhammad (pbuh) insisted animals were well treated.
- If a man unjustly kills an animal he will be accused by the animal on Judgement Day (Sunnah).

Hinduism

- Avoid harming all forms of life (ahimsa).
- Hindu worship includes respect for all and many deities are linked to specific animals.
- By avoiding harm to animals humans will come to be ready for eternal life (Laws of Manu).
- It is the duty of the householder to feed animals.
- 'On a Brahmin … cow … elephant … dog … wise men look with an equal eye' (Bhagavad Gita).

- Remember you only need to look at the religion(s) you have been taught.
- Remember to APPLY the teaching to the question after you have stated it – see page 4 for guidance on this.
- For most answers probably three specific teachings plus the generic ones will be sufficient.

A useful revision technique: memory cards

This revision technique is really good for proving to your parents that you are doing some revision! Make memory cards – they should be about double business card size, so they are big enough to get a decent amount of information on, but small enough to go in a pocket (for that 'out-of-the-blazer-pocket-to-get-some-quick-revision-in-the-lunch-queue' moment!).

Suits all learners

Those of us who are kinaesthetic learners will enjoy the making, and then the handling of the cards. The reducing and writing of detail, along with the spoken element of using these cards, suits audio learners. Meanwhile the look of them aids visual learners.

Mix and match

You can make cards that have set questions on them, for example asking how people use animals in sport. You could put images which have a question or statement stimulus, for example a picture of someone with a guide dog, and the statement 'It is wrong to make animals work for us'. You should have cards that ask for religious attitudes, for example religious attitudes to animal experimentation – **should** because this is an RS exam, and if you want the better grades, you have to provide the religious ideas.

Using the cards

Simple! Read side one, think of or say your answers, then check side two. Or get someone to read/show you side one, and you give them the answers from side two (that's where your parents come in handy!). If you have rewritten the side one question at the top of side two, before the answer, then you can just read and reread that side to make yourself remember.

How do we use animals?

Companions, pets, helpers, beasts of burden, for hunting, in zoos, work animals, experimentation, for their fur, sport.

It is wrong to keep animals in zoos.

Zoos are bad because – unnatural environment and climate; animals can't be free; enclosures often too small; morally wrong.
Zoos are good because – breeding programmes; educate us; scientific knowledge can be gained.

Religious attitude to animals

Christian – God made them; humans have stewardship; must be kind to them (Old Testament); morally right to look after all of world including animals for the future of the world.
Buddhist – all part of cycle of rebirth; all life is sacred; principle of not harming which comes from First Precept – do not hurt any sentient being; let no one kill nor cause another to kill – Dhammapada.

What questions on this topic look like

This page contains a range of examples of questions that could be on an exam paper for this topic. Practise them all to strengthen your knowledge and technique while revising. Page 17 has answers to some of these, with tips.

Check back to pages 6 and 7 to see the grids that examiners use to mark questions worth three marks or more, to help you answer them.

One-mark questions
- What is meant by *animal rights*?
- What is meant by *vegetarian*?

Two-mark questions
- Explain what is meant by *animal rights*.
- Give two ways in which humans use animals.

Three-mark questions
- Explain why some religious believers think it is wrong to eat meat.
- Explain how humans and animals are different.
- **Animals should have the same rights as humans**. What do you think? Explain your opinion.

Four-mark questions
- Explain religious attitudes to animals. Refer to beliefs and teachings in your answer.
- Explain two ways in which religious people can work for animal rights.
- Explain religious attitudes to experiments on live animals. Use religious beliefs and teachings in your answer.

Five-mark questions
- Explain religious attitudes to using animals in farming. Refer to religious beliefs and teachings in your answer.
- Explain the ways in which humans make use of animals in the world today.
- Describe the food laws which religious believers might follow.

Six-mark questions
- Explain religious attitudes to the conservation of endangered species. Use religious beliefs and teachings in your answer.
- **Zoos should all be closed down**. Do you agree? Explain your reasons, showing you have thought about more than one point of view. Refer to religious arguments in your answer.
- **It is wrong to use animals in sport**. Do you agree? Explain your reasons showing you have thought about more than one point of view. Refer to religious arguments in your answer.

Did you know that F-grade candidates rarely use the correct technical terms in their exam? This means they can find some questions difficult just because they didn't know what the question was asking. If this sounds like you, make a list of words which are important, and make sure you learn them all.

Did you know that C-grade candidates use some of the technical words in their exam, but not as many as they could do? They might recognise the words when they are in the questions, but they don't answer with enough depth. Using the words makes your answers sound better, and usually means you will be sharper in what you are saying. Learn the words, and use them more often, so that they are part of your vocabulary anyway.

Did you know that A-grade candidates know and use the correct technical language all the time in their exam? This makes the exam easier, because they don't have to try to work out what the questions are asking. It makes their answers better, because they are sharper, sounding more knowledgeable. If this is you, add greater depth to your use of these questions, don't be satisfied with just knowing what they mean, learn examples and find out more detail about each one.

Which one are you? And how do you move to the next level?

Explain what is meant by *animal rights*. (2)

It means animals having rights like humans do. Like treating them properly instead of being cruel.

Animals should have the same rights as humans. What do you think? Explain your opinion. (3)

No, I don't agree. We rule the world, and animals can't do what we can. We build buildings, and make technology – animals can't. But you could say that we all live on this planet, so it is for us all to share. Also you could say that as we depend on animals we have to give them rights – it is only fair to treat them well.

Explain religious attitudes to experiments on live animals. Use religious beliefs and teachings in your answer. (4)

Christians say that God created the world and all animals too. This means their life is special and sacred. God gave us dominion over the animals - it says this in Genesis (Bible). This means we can treat them how we want to, but we should be stewards which means looking after. I think it means we can use animals but have to look after them. We are allowed to eat them, so I think we can do other things with them too.

Explain the ways in which humans make use of animals in the world today. (5)

We use them to do jobs like pulling carts and ploughing fields. Some ride horses maybe for fun, maybe as transport. Lots have pets like cats and dogs. The police use them to find drugs and dead bodies, and for bombs. My dad likes fishing.

Zoos should all be closed down. Do you agree? Explain your reasons, showing you have thought about more than one point of view. Refer to religious arguments in your answer. (6)

I agree because many zoos are cruel. The cages are too small for the animals, who usually have miles and miles to roam around in. Also the animals are from all over the world. This means that some of them are always in the wrong climate, so they'd be too hot or too cold all year. Lots of zoos have concrete compounds, so the animals aren't in their proper environment. You often see animals walking round and round, which means they are bored. I think all this proves it is cruel.

I disagree for some other reasons though. Lots of zoos now have breeding programmes, and if they didn't breed the animals then the animals would die out. So really they are helping the world – they let some of them back into the wild. Also it is important for people to see what is in the world. Most people couldn't afford to go and see polar bears, but if they saw them in the zoo, they might decide to give money to a charity to save polar bears from dying out. Kids learn from zoos about the rest of the world too, so that is good.

Exploring an exam question

A full exam question looks like this. It always has a stimulus, two AO2 evaluative questions, and two or three AO1 questions. The total is 18 marks, split equally between the two types of questions.

Look at the picture below. It shows different animals.

On your exam paper, all the questions will have the same number of parts. So if the first is split into four parts, then all the rest will be too. If the first is split into five parts, all the rest will be too. In this book we have given you examples of each.

Just list two

01 Give **two** ways in which humans use animals as helpers. (2)

Give a definition, then say a bit more to expand the definition, or give an example to show what you mean

02 Explain what is meant by *animal rights*. (2)

You could answer this from one point of view, but full marks are easier from two

03 Explain religious attitudes to animal rights. Refer to beliefs and teachings in your answer. (5)

You can answer from one or two religions, but must give beliefs/teachings to get higher marks

04 **Religious people should try to stop bull fighting across the world.** What do you think? Explain your opinion. (3)

Remember to argue from two sides, explaining all the points you make, and including some religious arguments. The statement is about eating meat, not about animals directly

05 **Humans should eat more meat.** Do you agree? Give reasons and explain your answer, showing you have thought about more than one point of view. Refer to religious arguments in your answer. (6)

Dewi gave the following answers. Read them to try to work out what is good about his answers, and what could be done better, then try to write perfect answers for him. There are some pointers on page 92. You could also use pages 6 and 7 to check the AO1/2 grids for how to answer parts **02**, **03** and **04** below.

01. Pets – old people like a friend like a cat, it keeps them company and that helps when you are old. Or to pull carts, so people can move heavy stuff around.

02. It means the rights that animals have, like humans.

03. I think Christians can use animals how they want to. They have 'dominion' over them from God – it says so in the Bible. Seeing as how God made everything, then they should look after them too.

Hindus really respect animals. They are nearly all sacred. Gods use them as vehicles, so that makes them special. The cows are most special though – you can't even kill cows in India, they even have retirement homes for them.

04. I think they should because it is cruel to the bulls. They have to fight against someone who has to hurt them not kill them. Even when they win, they often die because of their wounds, or by bad treatment on their way to retirement. It is cruel.

05. I agree because there is so much meat thrown away and wasted. It is better for your health as well. I also disagree because where would we get it all? Hindus don't eat meat at all, so they wouldn't agree – the cow is a sacred animal. It depends what animal as well – more farm animal meat would be okay, but not animals like monkeys.

Religion and animal rights: thought map

This is a great revision tool. It gives the topic in the centre and builds it up to the detail in the outer reaches. Topics are split into elements (which are the chunks you study, sort of like the titles of different lessons on the same overall topic). Those elements are the layer after the middle. Then the elements are split into the areas that questions would focus on. Next layer out are the broad answers to those. Knowing it all to this layer is enough for the D grade. Finally, there are the detailed bits of the answers, which is where you get your higher grades.

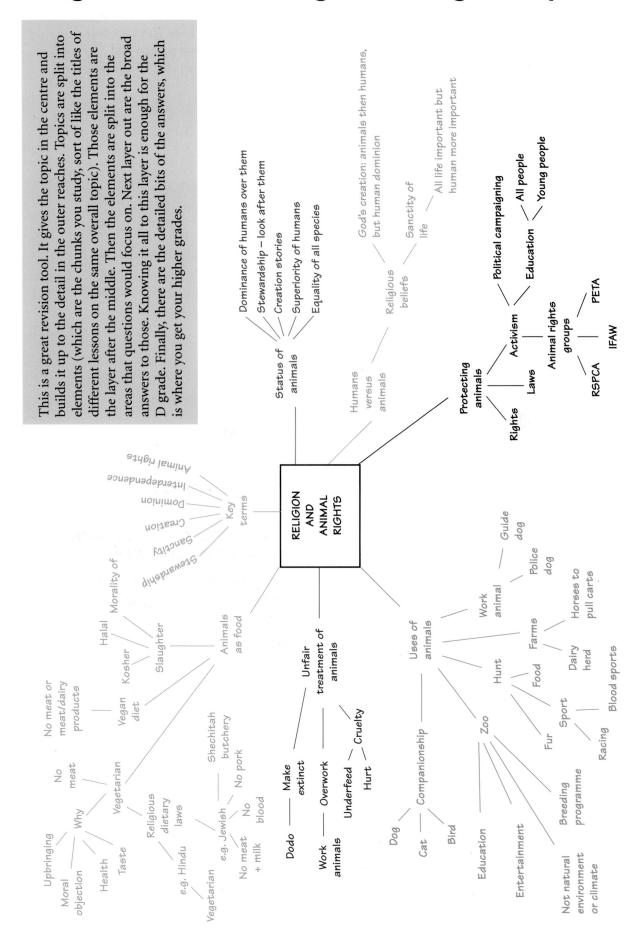

Status of animals
- Dominance of humans over them
- Stewardship – look after them
- Creation stories
- Superiority of humans
- Equality of all species

Humans versus animals
- Religious beliefs
  - God's creation: animals then humans, but human dominion
  - Sanctity of life
  - All life important but human more important

Protecting animals
- Rights
- Laws
- Activism
  - Political campaigning
  - Education
    - All people
    - Young people
- Animal rights groups
  - RSPCA
  - IFAW
  - PETA

Key terms
- Stewardship
- Sanctity
- Creation
- Dominion
- Interdependence
- Animal rights

RELIGION AND ANIMAL RIGHTS

Morality of
- Halal
- Kosher
- Vegan diet
- Slaughter
  - Shechitah butchery
  - No pork
  - No blood

Animals as food

Vegetarian
- Why
  - Upbringing
  - Moral objection
  - Health
  - Taste
- Vegetarian
  - No meat
  - No meat or meat/dairy products
- Religious dietary laws
  - e.g. Hindu
  - e.g. Jewish
    - No meat + milk

Unfair treatment of animals
- Make extinct — Dodo
- Overwork — Work animals
- Underfeed
- Hurt — Cruelty

Uses of animals
- Work animal
  - Guide dog
  - Police dog
  - Horses to pull carts
- Farms
  - Dairy herd
  - Food
- Hunt
  - Sport
  - Blood sports
  - Racing
- Zoo
  - Fur
  - Education
  - Entertainment
  - Breeding programme
  - Not natural environment or climate
- Companionship
  - Dog
  - Cat
  - Bird

Religion and animal rights: revision checklist

Go through the words and ideas on this page. They are the key ideas for this topic. For each word and each idea colour or mark it 'Know it' (green), 'Know a bit' (yellow), or 'Know little' (red). You then know which bits you have to spend most time on in your revision (the reds), and which ones are the easiest to remember but also the most tempting to revise again (green). This gives you a guide to focus and prioritise your revision.

Key words to learn ✓

Animal experimentation

Animal rights

Cloning

Companionship

Creation

Extinction of species

Factory farming

Fur trade

Genetic engineering

Hunting

Ivory trade

Sanctity of life

Stewardship

Vegan diet

Vegetarianism

Zoos

Subjects within topic – do you know? ✓

✦ How humans use animals to help them

✦ How humans exploit animals

✦ How humans and animals differ – the status of each

✦ Religious attitudes to animal rights

✦ Religious attitudes to slaughter methods, to meat eating

✦ Food rules for a religion

✦ Religious attitudes to animal experimentation

✦ Religious attitudes to zoos, including their role in conservation of species

✦ Religious attitudes to uses of animals in sport, including hunting, bull-fighting and racing

✦ Religious attitudes to farming, including factory farming

✦ The 'rights and wrongs' of each of the ways humans use animals

Good luck on this topic!

21

Topic Two Religion and planet earth

Overview

For this topic, you need to know about:

- different ideas about the origins of life
- how the earth inspires awe and wonder in people
- ideas of care and responsibility for the planet (stewardship)
- how we look after the planet
- problems caused by pollution
- effects of modern lifestyles
- debate about and effects of climate change (global warming)
- use and abuse of natural resources
- destruction of natural habitats.

For each of these you need to be able to explain specific terms, give examples to show your understanding, explain why people may agree or disagree with the issues, write about problems associated with them, and give religious attitudes to them.

You also need to be able to evaluate (agree with and disagree with) statements about these issues.

Definitions of key terms

You could be asked to define any of these in the exam, or the phrases could be used in questions.

Acid rain – rain made acidic by being contaminated, for example by waste gases which get into the atmosphere from factories.

Awe and wonder – sense of respect and admiration, often linked with fear.

Carbon emissions – release of carbon dioxide into the atmosphere from many sources, e.g. power stations.

Conservation – looking after, preservation of the natural environment.

Deforestation – cutting down trees over extensive areas.

Destruction of natural habitat – actions which lead to the natural homes of plants and animals being destroyed, often leading to the deaths of those species.

Drought – lack of rain over an unusually long spell.

Earth summit – meeting between representatives of governments from all over the world to try to reach agreements about what can be done to look after the planet.

Famine – extreme scarcity of food, often because of the failure of harvests due to weather conditions.

Flood – influx or overflowing of water beyond its usual limits on to land, e.g. a river bursting its banks because of excessive rainfall.

Global warming – the heating up of the earth's atmosphere, leading to climatic change.

Greenhouse gases – gases in the earth's atmosphere. They allow the sun's rays to enter our atmosphere, but then trap them causing a heating effect.

Natural resources – the things we use which occur naturally, e.g. gas, oil, coal, wood.

Oil spills – where transported oil has been accidently spilled in large quantities on land or in the sea, destroying the environment.

Pesticides – chemicals used by farmers to kill insects.

Pollution – an excess of anything leading to environmental problems, e.g. an oil spillage leads to pollution in the sea which kills sea life.

Recycling – reusing something rather than just letting it become waste.

Severe weather – weather conditions which are extreme and not usual for the area, e.g. flooding.

Stewardship – sense of responsibility for the planet, for animals, for others; a duty to look after.

Sustainable development – project developments which meet the needs of today without compromising the needs of future generations.

Toxic chemicals – chemicals that are poisonous.

Topic basics 1 – 'The origins of life'

This topic is about the planet we live on so a good place to start the basics is: 'Where did it come from?' You need to learn both the scientific and religious explanations and arguments for and against them.

Science: the Big Bang

- 20 billion years ago – nothing.
- Huge explosion caused a cloud of dust and gas.
- Cloud settled to form the universe, and the planets in it.
- Earth was only mud – primeval soup.
- Proteins and acids in the mud fused together.
- Simple life forms began.
- Life developed into insects, birds, fish, reptiles and mammals.
- First human – five million years ago.

Think about these ideas
How can nothing explode?
What caused the explosion in the first place?
How can a cloud form the universe?
Where did the mud come from?
How can an explosion cause a perfect formation like the world – explosions usually cause chaos and destruction?

God and nature

Religions use the following ideas to support their belief in creation:

- The beauty, complexity, power, yet peace and calm of the world cannot be an accident, suggesting a creator – God.
- The world's design seems deliberate – so it must have a designer.
- How did it happen? Science can't explain why something that began with nothing suddenly became a place with the right conditions for life.
- The more you look at the beauty of the world, the sea's power, landscapes, the planets, sunsets, etc., the more filled with awe, wonder and questions you are.
- People are inspired by the world around them to think of God as there isn't any other explanation for it all.
- We must therefore respect this gift and worship God by looking after it.

So … what do religions tell us?

1 Creation
Christianity, Islam and Judaism have the same story:

- God created the earth from nothing in six 'days'.
- First, the world: air, water, land vegetation, sun, moon, stars and seasons.
- Then life: birds, fish and then land animals … finally humans.
- seventh day of rest: God was pleased and the world was good.

Hinduism:

- Created by Brahman.
- Vishnu slept on a cobra in middle of nothingness.
- Vishnu wakes and lotus flower grows from his navel.
- Brahma is inside the lotus who creates the world.
- Shiva is also there to be responsible for the cycle of life and death.

Sikhism:

- God created the world. Without God nothing exists.
- God keeps life going.

2 Stewardship
- The world belongs to God so we should look after it.
- Looking after the world shows respect and gratitude and is a duty to keep.
- It's like an act of worship to look after God's world.

3 The future
- If I ruin the world I have to live in the mess.
- So do others and our children.
- God will reward me if I look after his world, but punish me if I don't.
- Hindus, Buddhists and Sikhs believe in reincarnation and that they will need the world again.

Topic basics 2 – The earth's problems

The issues

There are a number of problems and issues that affect the earth which you need to be aware of as well as some of the solutions to these problems. There are also some key terms here that you need to know. For the exam, be able to say what the issue is; why it is happening; problems raised by it; and possible solutions.

Pollution

Pollution is where too much of something has caused an imbalance and damage to the environment. It is something usually dumped into the water or land or released into the air. It is usually a dangerous substance. Some examples include:

- Acid rain (rain made acidic because of air pollution from factories and power stations) which damages buildings.
- Oil spills from tankers which kill birds and sea life.
- Toxic chemicals spilled into rivers and on land, sometimes caused by a build-up of pesticides from farms.

Problems

- Rivers and waterways become contaminated – fish die or we eat them.
- Land is covered with litter and landfill dumping sites.
- Air is polluted by factories, cars, noise – this affects human health.
- Beaches and the sea are polluted with sewage.

Solutions

- Cut the level of toxic waste.
- Recycle rubbish.
- Use cars and planes less often.
- Governments can make world agreements to cut carbon emissions.
- Use of cleaner fuels.

Global warming

'Climate change' is another phrase for this because global warming is happening as a result of climate change. Scientists tell us that the earth's temperature is getting hotter because greenhouse gases are allowing the sun's rays into our atmosphere but then trap them. This can have dire consequences for humans, animals and the natural world on earth and under the sea.

Effects/problems caused

- Ice caps melting causing seas to rise and land to disappear under the sea.
- Severe weather patterns – floods and droughts – leading to destruction of crops and famine.
- Sea life/reefs dying as sea temperature and depth changes make the conditions wrong for the life in those areas.
- Animal's habitats being destroyed as climatic change happens, e.g. polar bears are now threatened because the ice flows they need to travel on are disappearing.
- Cancers are on the increase because more of the harmful rays from the sun are getting through the atmosphere to our level.

Solutions

- Using less energy such as through insulating our houses, switching off appliances, etc. Industries finding alternative and renewable energy sources.
- Creating more renewable energy sources with low-carbon emissions, such as wind farms and harnessing wave and solar energy.
- Creating less pollution through recycling more, using our cars less, reducing factory emissions, etc.
- Everyone – individuals, companies, and governments – taking responsibility for being part of the solution, including setting and hitting targets.

Destruction of natural habitats

Issues
Damage is being done to natural habitats by pollution and by direct human activity. Deforestation is an example of this:

- Deforestation is the removal of rainforests at a dramatic speed.
- Huge areas of trees have been cut down for building, mining and cattle grazing.
- Trees are good for the environment – they capture the carbon dioxide from the atmosphere and produce oxygen for us to breathe.
- Animal homes disappear – animals die and become extinct.
- Rainforests contain plants that we can use in new medicines and these will be lost.
- Here our actions damage or put at risk our own existence.

Solutions
- We have to balance humans needs for land with our use of the environment, because when trees or species have gone they can't return.
- International agreements to protect areas – creating national parks, for example.

Use and abuse of natural resources

Natural resources include vegetation, minerals and fossil fuels such as coal, gas and oil. Humans use fossil fuels very heavily – think how much we rely on coal, gas and oil for travel, heating and energy. So what are the problems, and what are the potential solutions?

Issues
- Fossil fuels are being used in greater amounts and at a faster rate.
- Increasing use of technology across more of the world means more use of energy and resources, that causes more pollution.
- A greater number of people travel more and further, using up more fuel and creating pollution.
- Natural resources such as coal and oil are running out because of the rate at which they are used. The earth took millions of years to produce them. We need to find other sources of energy which won't run out – and we need to switch to them.
- When oil runs out the world would cease to work as it does at the moment because we rely too heavily on it as a fuel and haven't set up alternatives in enough quantity.

Solutions
- To cut down on energy use.
- To create renewable energy such as wind power, solar power, wave energy – and things we don't even know about yet.

Modern living

It is easy to think that global warming and pollution are not our fault or are issues too big for us to deal with, but as individuals we put huge demands on the planet. We have to accept that modern life puts a big demand on the earth and its resources – fuel demands for all the technologies we use and for our travel; food we buy and waste; rubbish sites filling up, and so on. We have to think of the effect of the following issues.

Issues
- We have cars that produce polluting gases.
- We produce tons of rubbish as a family each year – food waste, packaging and so on.
- We use a great deal of energy.
- Most of our foods are grown with pesticides these poison the land.
- A lot of fast food comes from cattle grazed on land that was rainforest.

Solutions
- Take responsibility for our own contribution. If everyone did a little then collectively it would have a great effect. Walk more, recycle, turn off lights, take things off standby, eat organic, etc. Our use of these creates a 'carbon footprint', i.e. the amount of carbon we are each responsible for.

Topic basics 3 – Looking after the world

The issues

The work being done to look after the world includes international action such as earth summits and targets to reduce carbon emission and action involving sustainable development and conservation projects.

International action

Earth summits

- An earth summit is a meeting of governments from all over the world every ten years to discuss environmental issues.
- These summits make efforts to build agreements between nations.
- They look at environmental problems and particularly try to help poorer countries to tackle the issues, as these countries have too little money, but need to develop quickly for the benefit of their people.

Target Setting – Kyoto

- In 2002 at the earth summit in Kyoto, Japan, many governments agreed to sign up to set targets for the future in order to:
  - use cleaner power more – wind, solar, wave energies
  - reduce the amount of carbon dioxide emissions.
- If these agreements are kept they will have a positive impact on reducing global warming, because actions make the difference not just agreements.

Sustainable development

Sustainable development is at the heart of the earth summits, and all the agreements made at them. Governments have to find technological advances and energies which can still exist and benefit people of future generations. It is no good swapping one resource which will run out for another one which will also run out. It is wrong to use up all the resources, and leave nothing for the future. It is also wrong to expect the poorest countries to pay the highest prices to make life better for their people now – they need to be helped by the richer countries.

Conservation

- Conservation is the idea of protecting an area or species.
- It could be action to repair a damaged area, such as planting trees, or to protect an area such as starting up nature reserves, etc.
- Conservation can be the work of governments, organisations or individuals (such as taking a holiday to work for an environmental project).

What about you … ?

Individuals could:

- Make small changes to their lifestyle to save energy.
- Adopt animals in nature reserves.
- Recycle more.
- Join an environmental organisation – Greenpeace for example.
- Pray for people to work together.

Topic basics 4 – Religious attitudes to planet earth

Remember you only need to learn the teaching(s) from the religion(s) you have studied.

Christianity ✝

- God gave us the world and the responsibility to look after it. Many Christians actively campaign to 'heal the world'. Humans do have a special role as the earth is a great gift that God has entrusted to us.
- We also have a responsibility to each other, the poor of the world and our future children to make sure the world is still intact for many generations to come.

Buddhism ☸

- Buddhists believe that all life should be respected and as we will use the earth during many lifetimes it makes sense that we should all look after it. We protect it for ourselves as well as for our children.
- Buddhists believe that it is ignorance and greed that lead to most of the pollution being caused – companies building factories in the developing world so they can pay their workers less, have fewer pollution controls to follow and make bigger profits. Ignorance and greed also stop people from reaching enlightenment – so it's double damage!

Hinduism ॐ

- Brahman is in all life. Hindu life began many years ago and was linked to a simple existence living on the land. The ideas of sanctity of life and non-violence became built into the religion.
- All life is interdependent – plants and animals and all life depend on their environment so everyone needs to protect it. All souls will be reborn so will return to the earth again and if God is in all nature then we show an act of worship by looking after it.

Judaism ♏

- After creating the world G-d gave us the duty of stewardship. We should respect it. Land left fallow on a regular cycle has always been in Jewish beliefs. Tikkun olam (repairing the world) is interpreted as tackling environmental issues; tzedek (justice) means justice for all animals and the world itself. To 'love your neighbour' you have to not wreck the world.

Islam ☪

- The world is the work of Allah – humans are khalifahs (stewards) and by being so show respect to Allah. We are trustees of his world – Allah knows who damages his creation and punishment will follow on Judgement Day. The idea of the ummah means we have a duty to pass on the world to the next generations.

Sikhism ☬

- The world is a gift from God – it only exists because God wants it to. Sikhs believe that the world is in a 300-year cycle so we must look after it. Sikhs perform Sewa for others so safeguarding the world is essential. For example, if we help the world's poor we help the environment.
- The Gurus said God is within everything so damage the world – damage God.

Religious teachings: good specific teachings to learn

Buddhism
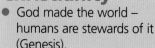
- First Precept is to not harm.
- Conservation is about our own survival not just about morality (Dalai Lama).
- The earth is not just our heritage but our ultimate source of life (Dalai Lama).
- Destruction of nature results from greed, ignorance and a lack of respect for the earth's living things – this shows a lack of respect to future generations (Dalai Lama).
- Compassion should be the centre of all actions.

Sikhism
- The universe comes into being by God's will (Guru Nanak).
- In nature we see God and in nature we hear God (Adi Granth).
- God created everything (Guru Nanak).
- Respect for all life.
- The Sikh ideal is a simple life free from waste.

Christianity
- God made the world – humans are stewards of it (Genesis).
- The earth is the Lord's (Psalms).
- More than ever people are responsible for the planet's future (Pope John Paul II).
- Jesus said love your neighbour.
- Respect for life extends to all of creation (Pope John Paul II).

All religions teach: creation, stewardship, awe, community and conservation

Judaism
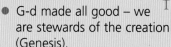
- G-d made all good – we are stewards of the creation (Genesis).
- The Torah speaks of not wasting so we should conserve resources.
- The earth and everything in it is the Lord's (Ketuvim).
- All I created for you. Do not corrupt or desolate my world, there will be no repair to it (Midrash Ecclesiastes Rabbah).
- Love your neighbour as yourself (Leviticus).

Islam
- The world is green and beautiful – Allah made you Khalifahs over it (Qur'an).
- The world was created as a place of worship (Qur'an).
- The earth has been created as a mosque (Hadith).
- Muhammad (pbuh) gave the example of not wasting nature – water was his example.
- Even on Doomsday a palm shoot should still be planted (Hadith).

Hinduism
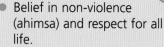
- Belief in non-violence (ahimsa) and respect for all life.
- Hindus should focus on environmental values (Artharva Veda).
- Trees give fuel, shade, a resting place, shelter to birds and medicines – this is their daily sacrifice (Varaha Purana).
- All life is interdependent – humans, animals and plants.

- Remember you only need to look at the religion(s) you have been taught.
- Remember to APPLY the teaching to the question after you have stated it – see page 4 for guidance on this.
- For most answers probably three specific teachings plus the generic ones will be sufficient.
- Notice some teachings can be used across more than one religion.

A useful revision technique: revision for the ears

Lots of people like to have something to listen to. Some people revise better by listening – either just listening, or listening and reading at the same time. There are boring times, like the walk or the bus to school, when it isn't possible to read, but it would be easy to listen. So making a recording of your notes is a good way to use up time which you would normally lose for revision.

Before recording

Well, you have to have something to listen to! And it has to make sense as well. This is all part of the revision process.

1. You make some notes – you could even use the 'Topic basics' sections from this book as your starter. Make sure your notes are in good order, and that they make sense when you read them back to yourself.
2. Some of these notes might be in the form of mnemonics, or rhymes, or songs – these styles can be helpful to many people, because they give a rhythm for the brain to remember more easily. See page 71 for more about these.

Recording

3. Now you have to record them on to an MP3 player or some other recording device. Do that in a quiet room away from other people, that way you don't get embarrassed and mess it up. For some people having music in the background helps, and when they work in the exam the thought of the songs helps to trigger memories of what was being revised with the song. Make them short and snappy – just fifteen to twenty minutes for any one session. Your brain works well over that time, but then begins to flag – so anything beyond that you probably won't remember.
4. You could get someone else to do the recording for you – especially if you'd associate that topic with that person (again it helps the brain remember). If you and your friends decided this would work for you, why not each record a couple, then exchange? Cuts the work down for all.

Revising

5. Lastly, you listen to them as often as you can. Any normally 'dead' time is useful, on the bus to school, walking to school (your mates won't even realise it is revision you are doing!), eating your breakfast, getting to sleep even. In some schools, students are allowed to manage their own revision in classes – why not listen then?

Podcasts

If this is your thing, why not create and share your revision material with the world. Podcasts are audio broadcasts that can be accessed through the internet. You'll need special software (such as Audacity), but you can get that online for free. You create the audio, then publish it to web – loads of sites take podcasts. Some even pay you for it – hmmn, getting paid to revise, sounds interesting!

What questions on this topic look like

This page contains a range of examples of questions that could be on an exam paper for this topic. Practise them all to strengthen your knowledge and technique while revising. Page 31 has answers to some of these, with tips.

Check back to pages 6 and 7 to see the grids that examiners use to mark questions worth three marks or more, to help you answer them.

One-mark questions
- What is meant by *pollution*?
- What is meant by *stewardship*?

Two-mark questions
- Explain what is meant by *global warming*.
- Give two ways in which humans damage the world.

Three-mark questions
- Explain why some religious believers think it is wrong to destroy the natural environment.
- Explain how humans can look after the world.
- **Damaging the world is disrespectful to God**. What do you think? Explain your opinion.

Four-mark questions
- Explain religious attitudes to the use of natural resources. Refer to beliefs and teachings in your answer.
- Explain two ways in which religious people can work for the conservation of the planet.
- Explain religious attitudes to the environment. Use religious beliefs and teachings in your answer.

Five-mark answers
- Explain religious attitudes to destruction of the environment. Refer to religious beliefs and teachings in your answer.
- Explain the ways in which governments have worked to help the planet.
- Describe the ways in which modern living is putting pressure on the environment.

Six-mark answers
- Explain religious attitudes to the problem of climate change. Use religious beliefs and teachings in your answer.
- **Climate change is the biggest problem for humans**. Do you agree? Explain your reasons, showing you have thought about more than one point of view. Refer to religious arguments in your answer.
- **Religious people should do the most to look after the planet**. Do you agree? Explain your reasons showing you have thought about more than one point of view. Refer to religious arguments in your answer.

Did you know that F-grade candidates usually write very little? They usually only give one idea in any answer. They know only a bit of everything they need to know.

Did you know that C-grade candidates write quite a lot, but often not clearly making their points? They usually don't explain themselves consistently – sometimes they do, sometimes they don't. They know quite a lot about the subject, but not the details.

Did you know that A-grade candidates write lots? They explain most of the points they make. They use the religious words for things. They obviously know their stuff really well.

So, which are you?

Give two ways in which humans damage the world. (2)

Litter and cutting trees down.

Tip

Two correct ways – two marks.

Damaging the world is disrespectful to God. What do you think? Explain your opinion. (3)

I don't believe in God, so it can't be disrespectful to something that doesn't exist.

Tip

It is okay to make points like this – it is a valid argument against the statement. However, you will still need to do some more writing to get more marks. Always try to write three reasons for this type of question, and try to explain one of them.

Explain why some religious believers think it is wrong to destroy the natural environment. (3)

Because it belongs to God, because God made it, because it means lots of animals could die when their natural homes are destroyed.

Tip

The answer gives three reasons, but doesn't explain any of them; the question specifically asks you to do that. It would get two marks.

Explain religious attitudes to the environment. Use religious beliefs and teachings in your answer. (4)

Christians believe that God made the world and everything in it. He did this in the seven days of creation that is in the Bible. This makes the world special – it is God's creation. People should look after the world because it is God's not theirs. God made them stewards of the world, which is a duty to look after it. So they have to try to help the environment, because God will reward them after they have died.

Tip

This answer gives a good outline of the basic Christian attitude to the environment. It uses key technical words, like creation and stewardship, and is written in one flowing paragraph. It is worth full marks.

Describe the ways in which modern living is putting pressure on the environment. (5)

Humans take too many natural resources, like oil, gas, coal. They are running out because of that. So many cars everywhere makes too much pollution, and that is bad for the planet and for everyone's health. We waste too much, and don't recycle enough.

Tip

This is a good start to an answer, and would get three marks. What the answer needs is more development of the points, applied back to the question. How does modern living lead to the taking of too many natural resources, for example? What do we waste, and why do we do it? Extending the points you make will get you more marks.

Climate change is the biggest problem for humans. Do you agree? Explain your reasons, showing you have thought about more than one point of view. Refer to religious arguments in your answer. (6)

No it isn't. Wars and murders and paedophiles are. Climate change isn't making any difference to me or my life. If it makes the weather hotter, I'm glad, but I didn't notice that yet. You could say it is though because if the scientists are right, we need to worry a lot. They say the change will make the ice caps melt, and then the seas will flood countries. Cities like London and New York will be under the sea, like Atlantis went. Religious people might think that the number of not religious people in the world is the biggest problem.

Tip

This gives two sides, and a little bit of development of the points. Its big problem is that it jumps about so doesn't clearly make one point of view, then the other. By focusing your answer into one side, you can make sure of explaining your points clearly, then you can do the same for the other side. The answer has a religious argument in it – even if it isn't developed. This is worth three marks.

Exploring an exam question

A full exam question looks like this. It always has a stimulus, two AO2 evaluative questions, and two or three AO1 questions. The total is 18 marks, split equally between the two types of questions.

Look at the picture below. It shows young people making an environmental protest.

On your exam paper, all the questions will have the same number of parts. So if the first is split into four parts, then all the rest will be too. If the first is split into five parts, all the rest will be too. In this book we have given you examples of each.

You need to give a definition and then extend it

06 Explain what is meant by *global warming*. (2)

What other problems could be classed as 'biggest'?

07 **Global warming is the world's biggest problem.** What do you think? Explain your opinion. (3)

You'll need to give at least three teachings here about the environment and looking after it, which you then apply to the topic of pollution

08 Give **two** ways in which people damage the world. (2)

Make sure you answer about 'damaging' the world, not helping it

09 Explain religious attitudes to pollution. Refer to beliefs and teachings in your answer. (5)

What other duties do or should they have, and how do they compare? Must give more than one point of view. Can't get more than three marks if you don't refer to religious arguments

10 **A religious person's first duty should be to look after the world.** Do you agree? Give reasons for your answer, showing you have thought about more than one point of view. Refer to religious arguments in your answer. (6)

Stevie gave the following answers. Read them to try to work out what is good about his answers, and what could be done better, then try to write perfect answers for him. There are some pointers on page 92. You could also use pages 6 and 7 to check the AO1/2 grids for how to answer parts **07**, **08** and **09** below.

06. It means the world is heating up, so ice caps are melting, and the sea levels will rise and then there will be flooding and land will be lost, even London.

07. I think it isn't. I think that wars are worse, for those people in them. No point worrying about global warming if you are going to get blown up or shot before global warming happens really.

08. Litter and cutting down trees.

09. Religions don't like pollution because it damages the planet. They think we have to look after the planet as a duty, and that it will come back on us if we don't. Our children will have a worse world than we have, and that isn't fair on them. Pollution also makes the world look bad, like when streams have all rubbish in them. I went surfing and the rubbish made it really horrible sometimes.

10. I agree because we only have one world, and like I just said in my last answer, if we don't look after it it gets too badly damaged. We have to look after it for the next generations – I don't like it when I get given secondhand stuff and stuff that is broken, so I don't think our kids will thank us if we don't look after the world. Religious people have to be stewards and look after the world. That is a duty for them from God. I also disagree though because religious people must have to pray and worship before they do anything else. They wouldn't be religious if they didn't do all that praying, and they only look after the world because God told them to when they were worshipping him.

Religion and planet earth: thought map

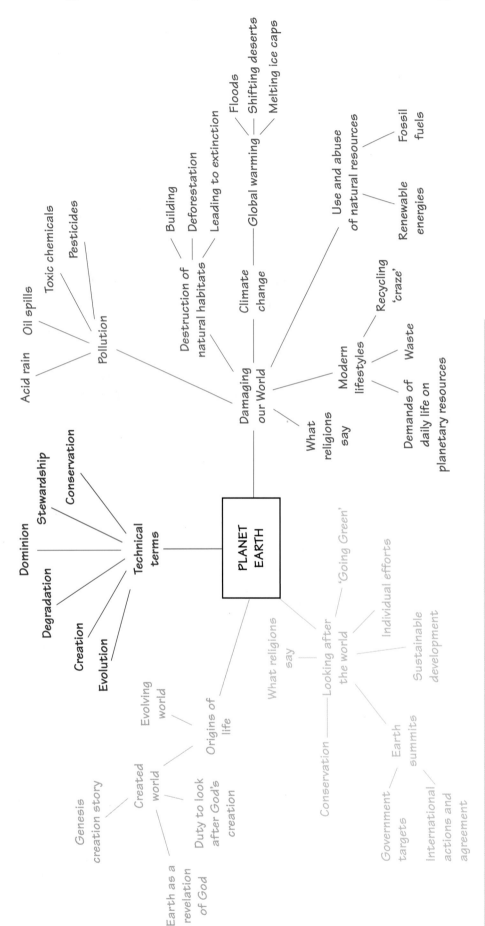

This is a great revision tool. It gives the topic in the centre and builds it up to the detail in the outer reaches. Topics are split into elements (which are the chunks you study, sort of like the titles of different lessons on the same overall topic). Those elements are the layer after the middle. Then the elements are split into the areas that questions would focus on. Next layer out are the broad answers to those. Knowing it all to this layer is enough for the D grade. Finally, there are the detailed bits of the answers, which is where you get your higher grades.

Religion and planet earth: revision checklist

Go through the words and ideas on this page. They are the key ideas for this topic. For each word and each idea colour or mark it 'Know it' (**green**), 'Know a bit' (yellow), or 'Know little' (**red**). You then know which bits you have to spend most time on in your revision (the **reds**), and which ones are the easiest to remember but also the most tempting to revise again (**green**). This gives you a guide to focus and prioritise your revision

Key words to learn ✔

Awe

Climate change

Community

Conservation

Creation

Earth summits

Natural habitat

Natural resources

Pollution

Renewable energies

Stewardship

Sustainable development

Subjects within topic – do you know? ✔

✦ Religious explanations of how the world and life began

✦ How the planet can be a source of awe and wonder making us think of God

✦ The problem with trying to help humans, but still protecting the environment

✦ How people damage the environment

✦ How and why people help the environment, both as individuals and in groups

✦ The world's response to environmental problems, e.g. earth summits such as Kyoto

✦ Religious attitudes to the natural world

✦ Religious attitudes to climate change

✦ Religious attitudes to pollution

✦ Religious attitudes to the use and abuse of natural resources

✦ Religious attitudes to the destruction of natural habitat

✦ Religious attitudes to conservation

✦ How modern living contributes to environmental problems, and how it needs to be part of the solution

Good luck on this topic!

Topic Three Religion and prejudice

Overview

For this topic you need to know:

- types of prejudice
- causes and origins of prejudice
- how people show prejudice
- effects of prejudice and discrimination
- religious attitudes to prejudice and discrimination
- concepts of tolerance, justice, harmony and the value of the individual
- responses to prejudice and discrimination: law, society, individuals and groups
- religious believers who have fought prejudice, e.g. Martin Luther King Jr, Mahatma Gandhi and Desmond Tutu.

For each of these you need to be able to explain specific terms, give examples to show your understanding, explain why people may agree or disagree with the issues, write about problems associated with them, and give religious attitudes to them.

You also need to be able to evaluate (agree with and disagree with) statements about these issues.

Definitions of key terms

You could be asked to define any of these in the exam, or the phrases could be used in questions.

Ageism – discrimination on the grounds of being old, middle-aged, young (age).

Community – people who work and live together so that everyone benefits.

Discrimination – putting prejudiced thoughts into action.

Equality – where everyone has the same value and importance.

Harmony – to live peacefully with understanding and respect.

Homophobia – discrimination on the grounds of sexuality (gay and lesbian people).

Justice – to treat people fairly.

Positive discrimination – benefits given to those who usually face negative discrimination.

Prejudice – pre-judge someone without evidence (negative thought).

Racism – discrimination on the grounds of colour of skin (race).

Religious prejudice – prejudice on the grounds of faith or belief, which can lead to discrimination.

Sexism – discrimination on the grounds of being male or female (gender or sex).

Tolerance – to accept people's differences.

Useful terms

Minority rights – small groups within society are called 'minority groups'; laws exist to give these groups protection and rights because they are often discriminated against by larger groups.

Multiculturalism – racial/social harmony brought about by having many cultures within society who understand and accept each other.

Race Relations Act – a law that made discrimination on the grounds of race illegal, and which stated that it was important to promote harmony and diversity between different ethnic groups for the benefit of all.

Topic basics 1 – What are prejudice and discrimination?

The exam often asks questions about what key words mean, such as prejudice, discrimination, racism. It also often asks why people become prejudiced, and how they show it. This topic basics tries to tackle those questions.

Types of prejudice

There are many different types of prejudice, and some are focused on in the exam:

- Racism, e.g. calling someone names because of their colour.
- Sexism, e.g. refusing someone a job because of their gender.
- Ageism, e.g. not listening to someone's opinion because of their age.
- Homophobia, e.g. someone being attacked because the attacker thinks they are gay.
- Religious prejudice, e.g. killing people of a certain faith because of what they believe.

Learn the definition of each of these (see page 36) and an example of it in action. This will help you answer one-, two- or three-mark AO1 questions.

Effects of discrimination

Discrimination can affect people/society in different ways, such as:

Negative
- Emotional – feeling left out, different, depressed, suicidal.
- Isolation within a community.
- Physically driven out of a community.
- Loss of property or possessions.
- Sense of total injustice.
- Actual death, as the most extreme form of discrimination is murder.

Positive
- Feelings of determination, not giving in, proud of who they are.
- Sense of community as people fight together against discrimination.
- Sense of purpose.
- Can provide jobs and support to people under-represented in areas of society, e.g. positive recruitment drive for gays in the police force.
- Balancing up society.

Causes of prejudice

Here are some of the main causes of prejudice:

- Upbringing – parents' attitudes against a certain group are also believed by their children, so that the children behave in an unfair way towards that group of people.
- Bad experience – a bad experience with someone from a certain group may affect a person's attitudes to others in the same group, leading to the belief 'They are all like that'.
- Media – biased coverage of an event may make someone form prejudiced attitudes, because they believe what the media said and take it as true for everyone in that group.
- Ignorance – judging someone or a group in a negative way without any actual real knowledge about them.
- Scapegoating – blaming others as an excuse for a problem, e.g. Hitler blaming the Jews for economic problems in Germany before the Second World War.

Learn to list each cause, say what they mean and give an example.

How discrimination is shown

Discrimination can be shown many ways, such as:

- Verbal, e.g. making a discriminatory comment or a joke, etc.
- Physical, e.g. violent action towards a person, even to the point of murder.
- Abuse of property, e.g. negative graffiti slogans.
- Discrimination by action, e.g. not employing someone, shunning someone or bullying.

Concepts

There are several key religious concepts that you should use in your answers to questions on this topic. Check the definitions on page 36 for these words:

- Justice, e.g. laws are designed to keep society fair; where there is an issue (injustice) then the law exists to make it right (provide justice).
- Tolerance, e.g. people understanding why and how others are different, so that they are accepting of them.
- Community, e.g. everyone in the area working together for their joint good – a bad deed against one is a bad deed against the whole community.
- Harmony, e.g. different peoples living in friendship together, accepting and respectful of each other's differences.

Know what these terms mean (see page 36). Think of examples where they can be shown positively and negatively so you have ideas you can take into the exam already worked out – saves exam time!

The law

Many laws exist to protect people against unlawful discrimination. The main ones are:

- 1976 Race Relations Act – makes it illegal to discriminate because of race, nationality or ethnic background or to use abusive language about race or publish material to stir up racial hatred.
- 2000 Race Relations Amendment Act – amended the 1976 Act to protect people in the public sector, police and government. Stressed the need to promote harmony and diversity.
- 1975 Equal Pay Act – men and women have to be paid the same for the same job.
- 1975 Sex Discrimination Act – promoted equal opportunities for men and women, and made it illegal to discriminate on the grounds of gender.
- 2005 Disability Act – ensured equal access and opportunities for people with disabilities, making it illegal to discriminate against them.
- 2007 Sexual Orientation Act – promoted equality for gay and lesbian people, making it illegal to discriminate on the basis of sexual orientation.

Topic basics 2 – Points about prejudices

This gives you the different types of prejudice which the exam could focus on, and some valid points that you could use in your answers

Racism

- All religions believe it is wrong to discriminate because of colour or race.
- Religions teach either that God created all humans, or that all are on the same cycle of reincarnation – meaning all are equal.
- Holy books and leaders teach respect, harmony and tolerance of each other.
- Religions teach that people are equal and no group has lesser value than any other.
- However racism still exists and many religious people believe they have a duty to campaign against it.

Ageism

- The law is not ageist – limits are set for our own good, e.g. an age before which people are not allowed to marry so that they will be old enough to make such a huge decision properly.
- Ageism is not confined to any particular age – young people suffer from it, and so do the old.
- The elderly should be respected, they are wise and experienced so need to be listened to; holy books stress this.
- People have a duty to look after the old, to repay them for what they have given in their own lives; most religions stress this as a duty.
- The young are the future and their views should be valued.

Sexism

- Sexism mainly affects women who suffer from discrimination which comes from traditional practices.
- Religions state that everyone is equal.
- In some religious traditions women are prevented from leadership; some people regard this as sexist.

Role of women

- In most religions women are not allowed to have the same roles as men, particularly in leadership. They are seen as having 'equal but different' roles in the home, in the religion and in society.
- There is a debate about whether this is a form of gender discrimination or not – different religions view it differently.
- Men generally do have more rights and freedoms and choices than women.
- Can we impose our attitude that something is discriminatory if the person we see as the victim does not?
- Women could offer a different approach in leadership than men, so providing a more holistic leadership to religions.
- Women should be able to serve God at the highest level as a right.

Homophobia

- All religions believe it is wrong to be homophobic: gay and lesbian people should not be discriminated against.
- It is against the law in Britain to target homosexuals and religions agree with this protection.
- Many religions agree that it is wrong to be actively homosexual. This is because it is seen as unnatural as it is impossible for sex to lead to the conception of children.
- Unlike other forms of prejudice, many gay and lesbian people face little support from religions and families.
- In some holy books there are statements condemning homosexuality.
- Within society and religions, prejudice against homosexuals is changing as we see the growth of, for example, Christian denominations welcoming homosexuals (Quakers), and the status of civil partnerships providing equal rights to gay couples.

Topic basics 3 – Some other prejudices

There are some other kinds of prejudice which you might bring into your answers. This page looks at them.

Religious prejudice

Each religion declares it has the right way so there is potential for discrimination in that 'being right' can make you feel superior, and can make you look down on others who aren't the same. Many wars and wholesale persecutions have been because of religious prejudice, e.g. the Crusader wars against Muslims; Hitler's persecution of the Jews in the Holocaust; Catholic Christian persecution of Muslims in Yugoslavia; Muslim persecution of Christians in Iraq.

- People are free to practise their own religion within Britain, so the law protects them.
- It is against the law to discriminate because of religious symbols, clothing, actions. Generally religious people support this stance.
- Organisations have been able to ban the wearing of religious insignia where it is not a required part of the religion, e.g. British Airways banning Christians from wearing visible crosses while on duty.
- Most religious groups promote tolerance of others, because they promote peace and understanding of others.
- For some religious people, different religions are seen as being different ways to the same goal.
- Religious groups often argue with and against other religious groups, and violent clashes are in the news regularly, e.g. Hindus and Muslims fighting each other in India. There can also be arguments within religions, e.g. the Catholic and Protestant arguments in Northern Ireland in the last century.

Looks and lifestyle

- We should not be too eager to judge just on looks.
- It is character not looks that matter.
- People should always be given a chance.
- Religions might not agree with certain lifestyles but they should not discriminate, rather be tolerant and accepting.
- Help, understanding, tolerance, respect should be shown.

Disability

- Everyone is equal – God creates us in different ways.
- We are all valued despite our differences.
- People with disabilities can actually teach us many things about attitudes to life.
- Difficulties can be overcome, and most people with disability live full and fulfilling lives.
- Who are we to judge the quality of life of another?
- The 1995 Disabilities Act makes discrimination in this respect illegal; all religions would support this.

How religious people can respond to prejudice and victims of it

- Pray.
- Look to holy books to help – see what they say.
- Individuals can speak to religious leaders.
- Campaign for change.
- Petition local councils or government.
- Education – through school assemblies.

Tip

These are standard answers that *can be used in any topic* where the question asks you 'What can religious people do to help …' just choose those from the list that apply to the topic you are asked about and *make them relevant*, for example:

- Pray *for those who suffer from prejudice* (this addresses the question).
- See what the holy book says *about homophobia* (this addresses the question).

Topic basics 4 – Famous individuals

Questions are usually asked about how the individual you choose to write about worked to fight against prejudice. (Don't fall into the trap of simply giving a full life story!)

Martin Luther King Jr (1929–1968)

- Black Baptist minister in the USA in the 1950s and 1960s.
- Leader of the US civil rights movement.
- Used political speeches, sit-ins, marches, boycotts, etc. as a method of political pressure for change (all direct non-violent action).
- His actions were based on his Christian belief that God created us all equal.
- He was assassinated in 1968 but had gained many equal rights for blacks, and is now remembered in an annual holiday in the USA.

Successes – his legacy
- Segregation is now illegal in the USA.
- Equal civil rights for blacks and whites.
- Voting rights for black Americans and equality across every aspect of society as well as protection under the law.
- Set the ball rolling for future black leaders such as Reverend Jesse Jackson and President Barack Obama.

Mohandas K. Gandhi (1869–1948)

- In the 1890s he worked in South Africa for the rights of migrant Indian workers.
- Led a movement against the British Empire for Indian independence in the 1930s and 1940s.
- Used non-violent direct action in India, such as marches, boycotts and hunger strike.
- Also campaigned against the caste system in India, setting examples.
- Assassinated in 1948.

Successes – his legacy
- In 1914 the South African government accepted many of his demands for the Indian people, giving them greater rights.
- In 1947 British rule in India ended, and the country gained independence.
- People's attitudes began to change towards the caste system so that some groups within Hindu society completely accepted the 'Untouchables', and they came to have more rights under law.
- His non-violent values and methods have been used and drawn on by other campaigners (e.g. Martin Luther King Jr).

Archbishop Desmond Tutu (1931–)

- South African black archbishop.
- Fought against the apartheid system of segregation.
- Organised a non-violent struggle using marches, boycotts and petitions.
- Brought the issue of apartheid to worldwide attention, which helped to bring pressure on the government to end the system.

Successes so far
- Apartheid system dismantled.
- Elections held – first black president elected (Nelson Mandela).
- His work led to South Africa fielding international sports teams which included people of all races.
- Shown that injustice can be fought successfully in a peaceful way.

Religious teachings: good specific teachings to learn

Sikhism

- 'Using the same mud, the creator has created many shapes in many ways' (Guru Granth Sahib).
- Those who love God, love everyone.
- God created everyone so all are equal and deserve the same treatment and respect (Mool Mantra).
- The use of the langar suggests everyone is welcome – Sikh or not.
- 'God is without caste' (Guru Gobind Singh).

Buddhism
- Five Precepts state 'do not harm others or use harmful language'.
- Metta (loving kindness) should be used by all.
- Everyone is equal and welcome in the Sangha.
- Prejudice creates bad karma
- Compassion should be the centre of all actions.

Christianity
- God created all of us as equal.
- 'There is neither Jew nor Gentile, slave or free man, male or female. We are all one in Christ' (New Testament).
- Do to others as you would want others to do to you.
- Jesus said love your neighbour.
- In the story of the Good Samaritan the man is helped because he needs it, not because of who he was or wasn't.

All religions teach: respect, community, tolerance, justice, fairness, equality and harmony

Judaism
- G-d created all of us equal.
- The Torah tells Jews to welcome and not persecute strangers.
- The Nevi'im states to practise justice, love and kindness to all.
- Treat others as you wish to be treated.
- Jews should live in harmony with non-Jews.

Islam
- Difference was Allah's design so persecution is unjustified.
- Allah loves the fair minded.
- The Five Pillars apply to all.
- Muhammad (pbuh) allowed a black African man to do the call to prayer.
- In Madinah all were welcome regardless of wealth, status or creed.
- The Muslim Declaration of Human Rights states all people are equal.
- On Hajj everyone is equal in dress and action.

Hinduism
- Belief in non-violence (ahisma) and respect for all.
- Compassion is a key belief with the desire to improve things for others.
- Hurting others can lead to bad karma and rebirth.
- Everyone has an atman so all are equal.
- The Bhagavad Gita states to reach liberation you should work for others.

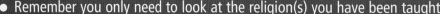
- Remember you only need to look at the religion(s) you have been taught.
- Remember to APPLY the teaching to the question after you have stated it – see page 4 for guidance on this.
- For most answers probably three specific teachings plus the generic ones will be sufficient.
- Notice some teachings can be used across more than one religion.

A useful revision technique: thought maps

On this page is a revision technique. This gives you guidance in a method that works for many people. You should try it to see if it works for you. Don't just restrict this to RS. Remember you can use these methods across all topics.

Thought maps

How do you revise? Do you read page after page and hope it soaks in? Bad news folks: this is probably the worst way to learn. Now, would you like to be able to write everything about a topic on one page? You can now learn how! This can be the start of your revision as to what you have to learn; it could be as a reminder of what you already know and what still needs to be done. I'd use it for both.

Look at the completed thought map on page 48. This is how it is done. Remember this method equates to eight to twelve pages for a full RS GCSE – that is eight if you learn the minimum number of topics (four per course), twelve if you learn the maximum. Mentally it is much better than a whole book to wade through. Although we have done one for each topic for you it does help to produce your own (we all think in different ways) and you need to add more detail to what is in this book.

The method

1. Put the topic in the centre of a sheet of paper.
2. Around it at the first level are the chunks which make up the topic – that is all the little elements of the topic (the sub-headings from the 'Topic basics' sections would do). Put each in a different colour.
3. Split each of these topic areas into a bit more detail – (the bullet points making up the sub-heading information).
4. You can add as many layers to this as you wish. The further away from the centre that the layer is, the smaller the detail it gives.
5. If you are struggling to learn so much information keep it simple. The basic elements remembered will get you that C grade.
6. For the A-grade student – more layers!

So why do these work?

- They are visual – the mind is able to process the colours and remember linked material because they are joined by colour.
- It is logical and cuts down the reading.
- It focuses the mind on the essentials – not getting carried away in waffle!
- In the exam you can visualise these and they really help to remember the information.
- Try this: focus on the mind map for two minutes ignoring everything else around you. Don't let your mind wander. Cover the page with a blank sheet and now try and reproduce all you can remember in ten minutes. The majority of people can reproduce at least 75 per cent of the material.
- Revision is that simple – all you do in the exam is visualise it in the same way, write in sentences and success is yours!

Happy revising!

What questions on this topic look like

This page contains a range of examples of questions that could be on an exam paper for this topic. Practice them all to strengthen your knowledge and technique while revising. Page 45 has answers to some of these, with tips.

Check back to pages 6 and 7 to see the grid examiners use to mark questions worth three marks or more to help you answer them.

One-mark questions
- What is meant by *racism*?
- What is meant by *prejudice*?

Two-mark questions
- Explain what is meant by *religious prejudice.*
- Give two reasons why some people are prejudiced.

Three-mark questions
- Describe the work of an individual who has tried to end prejudice.
- Explain the effects of discrimination.
- **It is always wrong for religious people to be prejudiced**. What do you think? Explain your opinion.

Four-mark questions
- Explain why religious believers think prejudice is wrong.
- Explain religious attitudes to positive discrimination.
- Explain how religious believers could work to reduce prejudice.

Five-mark questions
- Explain religious attitudes to sexism. Refer to beliefs and teachings in your answer.
- Explain, using beliefs and teachings, religious attitudes to ageism.
- Explain why religious believers have tried to end prejudice.

Six-mark questions
- Explain religious attitudes to racism. Refer to beliefs and teachings in your answer.
- **It is impossible to stop discrimination**. Do you agree? Give reasons and explain your answer showing you have thought about more than one point of view. Refer to religious arguments in your answer.
- **Racism is the worst form of prejudice**. Do you agree? Give reasons and explain your answer showing you have thought about more than one point of view. Refer to religious arguments in your answer.

Did you know that F-grade candidates usually only give very short answers to questions? They give one idea and move on to the next question – whatever mark is available. If this is you, force yourself to give two answers every time. You will increase your marks (and that means your grade).

Did you know that C-grade candidates often only give a couple of ideas for each answer? They can give a range of ideas, and sometimes they explain those ideas, but don't do it consistently across all their answers. If this is you, make yourself stop and think when you make a point – always explain.

Did you know that A-grade candidates usually write in paragraphs, which means they automatically explain what they say?

So, which one are you?

Explain what is meant by *religious prejudice*. (2)

It is when you are prejudiced against someone because of their beliefs, like you think Christians are 'all Bible bashers'.

Describe the work of an individual who has tried to end prejudice. (3)

Martin Luther King Jr tried to get human rights for blacks in America. He marched in a big march, and was killed by a white man.

Explain how religious believers could work to reduce prejudice. (4)

They could have marches. They could do petitions to get the government to do something about prejudice. They could help people and not be prejudiced themselves, like letting anyone go to their religious building.

Explain religious attitudes to sexism. Refer to beliefs and teachings in your answer. (5)

Christians say it is wrong. They believe that everyone is equal, because God made them all from Adam and Eve. Jesus didn't discriminate against anyone – he was always friendly to people who weren't accepted in society, like lepers and women. So Christians have to follow Jesus' example if they want to be classed as Christians. Muslims say everyone is made by Allah, so the same. He created different kinds of people to show his power. If you are Muslim, you treat everyone like brothers.

Racism is the worst form of prejudice. Do you agree? Give reasons and explain your answer showing you have thought about more than one point of view. Refer to religious arguments in your answer. (6)

In some ways I agree because people get killed through racism. If you are being hassled by racists, it makes your life really awful. Racism is part of some really bad things in history, like the Holocaust was some kind of racism. Religious people would agree with me because they say God made everyone equal, and racism says you aren't.

In other ways I don't agree. If I am harassed because I am a woman, then I'd think sexism was the worst kind. Or if I was always picked on because I am Jewish, then I'd think religious prejudice was the worst. People who are victims always think that they have the worst deal.

Exploring an exam question

A full exam question looks like this. It always has a stimulus, two
AO2 evaluative questions, and two or three AO1 questions. Total is
18 marks, split equally between the two types of questions.

Look at the picture below. It shows a mixed-race couple.

*On your exam paper,
all the questions will
have the same number of
parts. So if the first is split
into four parts, then all
the rest will be too. If the
first is split into five parts,
all the rest will be too. In
this book we have given
you examples of each.*

*Must have at
least one example
to be able to get
full marks*

11 Explain, using examples, what is meant by racism. (3)

*This is not
about attitudes
to women*

12 **Religious prejudice is the worst kind of prejudice.**
    What do you think? Explain your opinion. (3)

*Don't discuss
discrimination*

13 Explain religious attitudes to sexism. Refer to religious beliefs
    and teachings in your answer. (6)

14 **Discrimination is always a bad thing.** Do you agree? Give
    reasons for your answer, showing you have thought about
    more than one point of view. Refer to religious arguments in
    your answer. (6)

*Think about when
it can be positive, to
use in your counter
argument*

Kerrie gave the following answers. Read them to try to work out what is good about her answers, and what could be done better, then try to write perfect answers for her. There are some pointers on page 92. You could also use pages 6 and 7 to check the AO1/2 grids for how to answer parts 12, 13 and 14 below.

11. Racism is prejudice because of someone's colour. It means a person thinks someone is not as good as them because they are from a different country or a different colour of skin. Some people have been murdered because of racism.

12. I don't think it is. I think that most people have been hurt or killed because of racism not religious prejudice. Martin Luther King Jr was shot because he was black, and he was getting American blacks more power. Some people even kill themselves because of that. I have never heard of someone kill themselves because of religious prejudice. You could say it depends - the victim of any kind of prejudice might think that they are suffering the worst I suppose.

13. Christians believe God created us all equally. Eve was made from Adam's rib, and they were both given the world. It is always wrong to discriminate because that hurts people, and Christians should 'love their neighbour'. In the hymn, it says 'He's got the whole world in his hands' - it doesn't say 'except for women', so sexism must be wrong, when it means that women are less valuable than men.

In Sikhism, they say God created everyone and everything - that makes it all equal. Sexism must be wrong because of that. There are no rules to say women can't lead the prayers or the diwan (unlike some kinds of Christianity which say women can't - sexism really). Leading the prayer is about how good a person you are and that you can say the Guru Granth Sahib correctly, not if you are male or female. That shows that everyone is equal - men and women are the same.

14. Yes:
   • If it means against people like paedophiles -they shouldn't get jobs with children, we should discriminate against them.
   • If you want to increase numbers of certain groups of people, like in the police to make the police force reflect our society.
No:
   • Because discrimination is when people get hurt, like discriminating against someone because they are black so you hit them.
   • Discrimination is just not fair (against religious idea of justice), so it must be bad.

Religion and prejudice: thought map

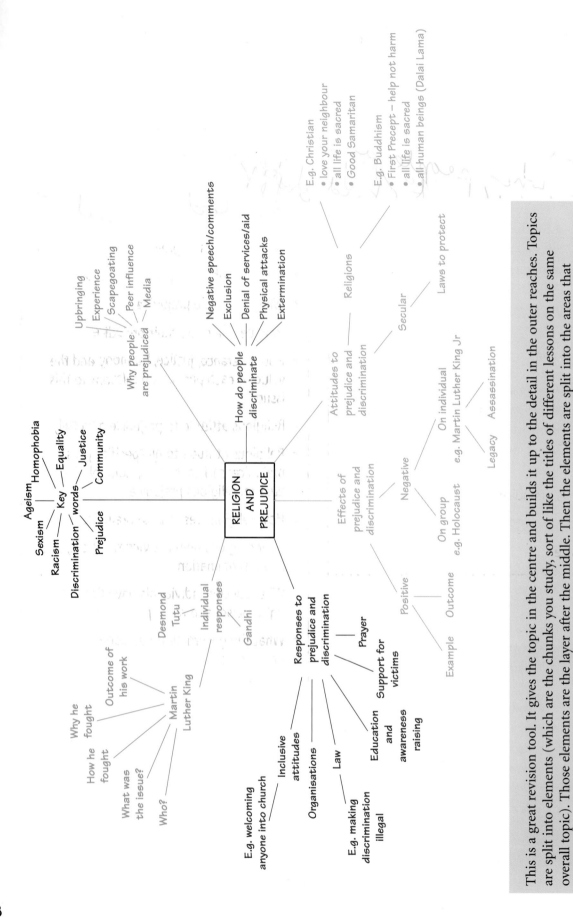

This is a great revision tool. It gives the topic in the centre and builds it up to the detail in the outer reaches. Topics are split into elements (which are the chunks you study, sort of like the titles of different lessons on the same overall topic). Those elements are the layer after the middle. Then the elements are split into the areas that questions would focus on. Next layer out are the broad answers to those. Knowing it all to this layer is enough for the D grade. Finally, there are the detailed bits of the answers, which is where you get your higher grades.

Religion and prejudice: revision checklist

Go through the words and ideas on this page. They are the key ideas for this topic. For each word and each idea colour or mark it 'Know it' (green), 'Know a bit' (yellow), or 'Know little' (red). You then know which bits you have to spend most time on in your revision (the **reds**), and which ones are the easiest to remember but also the most tempting to revise again (green). This gives you a guide to focus and prioritise your revision.

Key words to learn ✓

Ageism

Community

Discrimination

Equality

Harmony

Homophobia

Justice

Positive discrimination

Prejudice

Racism

Religious prejudice

Sexism

Tolerance

Subjects within topic – do you know? ✓

✦ Different types of prejudice: what they are

✦ Examples of each type of prejudice

✦ Why people are prejudiced

✦ How people show their prejudice

✦ How tolerance, justice, harmony and the value of each person are relevant to this issue

✦ Religious attitude to prejudice generally

✦ Religious attitude to all specific types of prejudice: racism, sexism, homophobia, ageism, religious prejudice

✦ How religions respond to prejudice

✦ How religions help the victims of prejudice and discrimination

✦ What specific individuals have done to fight racism and other prejudices

✦ What the government has done, e.g. the Race Relations Act

Good luck on this topic!

Topic Four Religion and early life

Overview

This topic is essentially about the issues surrounding abortion and the importance of life. For this topic you need to know about:

- The idea of the sanctity of life.
- Children as a gift of God, a blessing and a miracle.
- Issues about when life begins.
- Issues about the quality of life.
- Abortion and the rights of those involved – mother, father and the unborn child.
- Pro-Life and Pro-Choice groups and arguments.
- Religious attitudes for and against abortion.
- The law and abortion: the1967 and 1990 Acts.
- Adoption and fostering.

For each of these you need to be able to explain specific terms, give examples to show your understanding, explain why people may agree or disagree with the issues, write about problems associated with them, and give religious attitudes to them.

You also need to be able to evaluate (agree with and disagree with) statements about these issues.

Definitions of key terms

You could be asked to define any of these in the exam, or the phrases could be used in questions.

Abortion – deliberate expulsion of the foetus from the womb to terminate the pregnancy.

Adoption – to legally take on a child that is not your own.

Blessing – in the context of children being a blessing, the child can be seen as a gift from God to the parents.

Conception – when the sperm meets the egg in fertilisation.

Fostering – to temporarily look after a child that is not your own. It is still legally its mother's.

Miracle of life – the idea that becoming pregnant is so special – it's a miracle.

Pro-Choice – arguments focusing on the mother's right to choose an abortion.

Pro-Life – arguments focusing on the rights of the unborn child.

Quality of life – what a person's life should be like for it to be worth living.

Sanctity of life – life is special and sacred.

Useful terms

1967 Abortion Act – the UK law on abortion – had to be before 28 weeks of pregnancy with conditions.

Human Fertilisation and Embryology Act 1990 – the law that reduced the abortion limit to 24 weeks.

Topic basics 1

This page contains lots of bits: why people have children, when life begins and the law in the UK regarding abortion.

When does life begin?

- At conception when the sperm meets the egg.
- When it has a heartbeat at three weeks.
- When it begins to move – the quickening – at nine weeks.
- At birth when life is independent and can survive on its own.
- Some other time in between.

Why people want children

- To carry on family name and keep the religion going.
- It fulfils marriage promises and completes the family.
- The child is the expression of the love that the couple share.
- Religious duty to accept this gift of life from God.

Why people don't have children

- Too expensive.
- Not ready for the responsibility.
- Not in a stable or happy relationship.
- Too young or old or not in a position to care for a child.
- Medical reasons.

Key questions to think about

- Is abortion murder?
- Can you kill something which is not born?
- When is abortion not justified?
- Is it a necessary evil?
- Who should make the decision?
- Life of the mother versus life of the child?

Before 1967, abortion was illegal yet it still happened. There were around 100,000 cases a year and many women died as it was being carried out by unregistered people. Women were desperate and risked their lives to 'get rid'. So regulation was required.

The 1967 Abortion Act
States abortion is *illegal* in Britain, *but*:

- It can be carried out in specific circumstances where two doctors agree:
  - there is danger to the woman's mental or physical health
  - that the foetus will be born with physical or mental disabilities
  - that the welfare of existing children may be affected.
- The limit for an abortion to take place was 28 weeks. This was amended in 1990 to a 24-week limit. In reality, the majority of abortions take place within the first 12 weeks of pregnancy.
- It must be done by a registered doctor in a hospital or a clinic.

The Act opened abortion up to any woman who wanted one as it is difficult to think of any situation a woman might find herself in that would not fit into any of the three above clauses. As a result, there has been a massive increase in numbers of abortions and there is great debate as to the rights and wrongs of it.

Tip

Think about the questions on this page, because they form the main aspect of the statements you have to argue about in the exam – have some ideas already prepared. Remember it does not really matter what your personal opinion actually is – you just have to be able to have a variety of opinions in your mind to use.

Topic basics 2 – Arguments for and against abortion

This page outlines the arguments for and against abortion in what are called the 'Pro-Life' and 'Pro-Choice' stances.

The rights of the foetus (Pro-Life)

Pro-life arguments are totally against abortion and include the following:

- Life of the foetus is at least as important and for some more important than the life of the mother.
- The foetus must have someone speaking for it.
- All life has potential and should be given the chance.
- Abortion is murder – murder is wrong.
- All life is sacred and must be protected.
- God created all life so humans must protect it.
- A foetus should never be discarded as waste.
- We must not abort for a disability as we should not judge the quality of life of another.

You might be asked to briefly describe the work of a pressure group/organisation that works for the rights of the unborn child. Here is an example with ideas that you can use.

ProLife.org.uk
- Set up to secure the rights of all to life.
- Related to any issue of life – abortion, suicide, euthanasia.
- Believes in educating people – the right to life is the basic human right.
- Campaigns politically for law changes.
- Keeps the issues focused in the media.

The woman's right to choose (Pro-Choice)

Pro-choice arguments are based on the woman's rights to choose and the right to decide what happens to her body, including abortion. The arguments focus on the woman, not the foetus, and include the following:

- A woman has the right to decide what happens to her body.
- Some foetuses are so damaged it would be cruel to let them be born.
- If the woman's life is at risk she should have the right to abortion.
- Where rape has occurred then abortion has to be an option.
- The foetus cannot survive outside the womb until a certain point so it is not a life in its own right until that point.
- Women would have abortions anyway, just not safe ones.

You might be asked to briefly describe the work of a pressure group or organisation that works for the rights of the woman. Here is an example with ideas that you can use.

Abortion Rights (the national Pro-Choice campaign)
- Set up to secure the rights of women to have abortions.
- A woman is best able to decide whether to carry on with the pregnancy.
- Campaigns against restrictions in the law.
- Campaigns for better provision and women friendly NHS-funded abortion services.
- Uses petitions, public meetings and publications.
- Wants to stop doctors blocking abortion requests.

Topic basics 3 – Religious attitudes to abortion

Buddhism

- texts do not mention abortion
- believes that taking life is wrong and it begins at conception
- bad karma would be created because of the intention to harm
- the foetus' chance of paying back karma is taken away
- abortion is seen as violent, gives the foetus no rights and does not show compassion
- but abortion can lead to less suffering and so accept it on these occasions.

Christianity

- only God has the right to take life; after all he created it
- the Roman Catholic Church is completely against abortion – life must be protected
- Protestants accept it as a necessary evil – but don't like it
- abortion must be a last resort and after much careful thought.

Hinduism

- believe in the main that abortion is wrong
- brings bad karma and prevents the foetus' soul from working through a lifetime
- some scriptures say those who abort will be aborted many times themselves
- but allow it to save the woman's life.

Islam

- believe it is wrong but Muslim law does allow it – necessary evil
- humans destroy Allah's plans for life
- some Muslims believe the soul enters the foetus at 40 days and others believe this happens at 120 days, therefore before these times they would allow abortion as the foetus is seen as just blood and cells
- acceptable if a woman's life was at risk because her life is seen as more important.

Judaism

- accepts abortion for medical reasons
- a woman's life takes priority if it is in danger
- some rabbis would accept abortion if the mental state of the woman was endangered, for example in the case of rape
- if there is likely to be severe deformity abortion can be considered
- the foetus is part of the woman not a life in itself.

Sikhism

- does not agree with abortion as it interferes with God's creation
- no direct teaching, so up to individuals to make decisions
- seen as morally wrong as life starts at conception
- it is a form of murder as the intention is to destroy life
- abortion goes against the idea of not harming others and sewa (service to others).

Topic basics 4

These two pages cover the idea of the quality of life and how this affects attitudes to abortion. It also considers whose right it is to seek an abortion, and whether there are alternative choices.

Quality of life argument

'Quality of life' means what someone's life is like and is an argument used to support abortion. This is mainly true of abortion on the grounds of disability, because the argument is that the *disability affects the quality of life* of the person when born, and this is unfair. For example, a foetus that has been diagnosed as having a severe physical or mental disability, or a foetus that will never as a person be able to look after themselves.

However, this means *other people making judgements* on whether a life is worth living, because the foetus has no say, nor even a chance to experience life and be able to make the decision as to whether it is worth living or not.

Having said that, as a percentage of the number of abortions done, it is *rare to see an abortion requested because of disability* arguments. The people making the decisions are not trying to be cruel, rather to be compassionate to the foetus. The action is seen as a *necessary evil* – the kindest thing to do.

Questions focused around quality of life

If faced with a question about quality of life, use these ideas to write about for your argument: what if the foetus was blind and deaf, totally paralysed, had severe mental disability, and would need 24-hour care and many operations? In these cases we could say the abortion was the right choice because:

◆ it prevented suffering and/or early painful death
◆ the person would have no independence
◆ the person would not be able to enjoy life to the full
◆ the person would potentially be the victim of discrimination.

But:
◆ Have we the right to decide the quality of life of another?
◆ Many disabled people are able to enjoy and achieve in life.
◆ Do you miss what you never had, e.g. sight or hearing?
◆ Life should always be given a chance and medical science could help in the future.

You could also make the point that not all disabilities are so bad, and the system could be abused because for example a woman doesn't want a child with a cleft palate.

Whose right is it to choose?

This is often used as an evaluation question because it allows many agree and disagree answers. You could include the following:

- woman
- husband
- boyfriend
- parents
- religious leader
- doctor.

The circumstances the woman finds herself in makes a difference to your answer. For example, if she is living in very poor circumstances, or already had a child with disability. So does when and how the child was conceived. For example, is she was too young, or if she was raped. You need to be able to have ideas for and against the people in the list and think: 'What if … the woman was young, not married, still at school, religious, has health problems', etc.

There is often no right or wrong answers here; as long as your ideas are sensible and logical you will get marks.

Alternatives to abortion

The exam could ask you what other options are available to the woman. You need to think about the pros and cons of the alternatives.

- Keep it: all could work out well or mother could face severe problems looking after, loving or providing for the child.
- Choose to risk own life: both might survive. Mother might die leaving the child alone or be seriously ill for life.
- Fostering: chance to be looked after by natural mother some time later. Child is confused and feels given up on and unwanted. Foster family may not work out.
- Adoption: the child is brought up by a good family, but the child may want to find the real parents and may face problems of being unwanted.

These are just some suggestions to get you thinking. Remember there are no right or wrong decisions. Try to be open-minded and accept that there are different points of view. This position leads to much better answers. Don't just be blinded by your own thoughts because you have strong beliefs about this topic – this leads to poor unbalanced answers. Be careful.

Religious teachings: good specific teachings to learn

Buddhism
- The First Precept guides us to help, not harm, others and reduce suffering.
- Metta (compassion) – loving kindness should be used by all.
- Life is special and to be protected.
- Intention is all important, e.g. the reasons for abortion.
- Life begins at conception.

Sikhism
- Life begins at conception.
- All life is special and should be respected.
- God fills us with light so we can be born.
- God created us, gave us life and will take it away.
- Sikhs should not harm others.

Christianity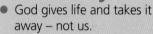
- God gives life and takes it away – not us.
- All life is sacred – special to God.
- All humans created in the image of God.
- God planned all our lives.
- The Ten Commandments say it is wrong to kill.

All religions teach: all humans have rights, life is special/sacred, protect life and people are all unique individuals

Judaism
- The foetus is as special as all life.
- Abortion under Jewish law is not murder.
- Emphasis is on life and new life not the destruction of it.
- We only gain full human status when we have been born.
- Until the fortieth day the foetus is 'mere water'.

Islam
- Life is sacred.
- Allah has planned our lives.
- We are all created from a clot of blood and known by Allah.
- It is wrong to kill.
- Allah decides the time of our birth and death.

Hinduism
- Belief in non-violence (ahimsa) and respect for all.
- Life is sacred.
- A woman who aborts her child loses her caste and karma is affected.
- Abortion is as bad as killing a priest or parents.
- Abortionists are among the worst of sinners.

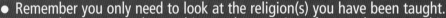
- Remember you only need to look at the religion(s) you have been taught.
- Remember to APPLY the teaching to the question after you have stated it – see page 4 for guidance on this.
- For most answers probably three specific teachings plus the generic ones will be sufficient.
- Notice some teachings can be used across more than one religion.

A useful revision technique: start with a plan!

Key principles

- Start early – three to five months before your exam starts – yes we know you don't like the sound of this but it does work.
- Starting early means it is a little at a time and you still have time for other things as well.
- Remember you have to fit in between possibly five and fourteen subjects.
- Use a diary, or design a rota of your free time after school.
- Start the first week setting aside perhaps half to one hour for revision. And as the weeks get nearer to the exam increase the time. Split each session up into slots of work so that when a slot is completed you feel like you have achieved something. This is better than simply reading a book and feeling overwhelmed by it.
- Perhaps think about one slot being a subject you don't like and the next being one you do like. (It is really easy to ignore what you find too difficult!)
- You must make sure you have a balance in your life or else it will be complete boredom and you will resent doing the revision.
- Give yourself goals. 'When I have finished this I can do something I like – read, watch TV, go out, play sport' … just time to relax and clear your mind. Overload is no good – you won't learn anything.
- Set a day at the weekend free (until you are within three weeks or so of your first exam). Have a complete change.
- Eat well and drink plenty of water – a hydrated brain learns better.
- Get plenty of rest and sleep.

See if your teacher will do a last-minute revision session either early in the morning before a morning exam or at lunchtime before an afternoon exam. This serves to focus the mind and get you thinking and alert.

If this idea would set you off in a panic of 'I can't remember anything!', then perhaps instead make sure you have some quiet time – a bit like a meditation. Some schools use this method before all their exams and surprisingly where they have, results have improved.

These are all just suggestions. Try some and see what works for you. Good luck!

What questions on this topic look like

This page contains a range of examples of questions that could be on an exam paper for this topic. Practise them all to strengthen your knowledge and technique while revising. Page 59 has answers to some of these, with tips.

Check back to pages 6 and 7 to see the grids that examiners use to mark questions worth three marks or more, to help you answer them.

One-mark questions
- What is meant by *abortion*?
- What is meant by *Pro-Choice*?

Two-mark questions
- Explain what is meant by *sanctity of life*.
- Give **two** reasons why some women choose to have an abortion.
- Give **two** reasons why some couples choose to have children.

Three-mark questions
- Explain ideas about when life begins.
- Describe what the law says about abortion.
- **Religious people should not have abortions**. What do you think? Explain your opinion.

Four-mark questions
- Explain why some religious believers might believe children to be a blessing on a marriage.
- Explain religious attitudes to having children. Refer to beliefs and teachings in your answer.
- Explain how beliefs about the quality of life might influence a person who is considering abortion.

Five-mark questions
- Explain why some religious believers disagree with abortion. Use beliefs and teachings in your answer.
- Using examples, explain why religious believers might agree with abortion. Use beliefs and teachings in your answer.
- Explain how the concepts of sanctity of life and quality of life can affect a person's decision regarding abortion.

Six-mark questions
- Explain attitudes to abortion. Refer to beliefs and teachings in your answer.
- **Abortion should only be available if a woman's life is in danger**. Do you agree? Give reasons for your answer, showing you have thought about more than one point of view. Refer to religious arguments in your answer.
- **A father should have the right to stop a woman having an abortion**. Do you agree? Give reasons for your answer, showing you have thought about more than one point of view. Refer to religious arguments in your answer.

Did you know that F-grade candidates often write very briefly? This is because they don't explain many of their answers. It is also because they don't use connectives to build longer sentences. If this is you, practise explaining yourself in every point you make.

Did you know that C-grade candidates write sentences and short paragraphs? They sometimes do and sometimes don't develop the points they make. If this is you, work on always explaining your ideas – this will give you fuller paragraphs and better marks.

Did you know that A-grade candidates usually write in detail and in good paragraphs? This is a characteristic of their work.

So, which one are you?

Explain what is meant by *sanctity of life*. (2)

It means life is special. God made it, so it is special.

Explain ideas about when life begins. (3)

People believe life begins at birth. Some religious people believe it is when the egg and sperm make the pregnancy start – at contraception. Some people think it is when you can feel the baby kicking.

Explain why some religious believers might believe children to be a blessing on a marriage. (4)

Religious people think that you should only have children if you are married. They think God gives the children to the couple – like a gift to them. So they only have a child because God has made it happen. This is a blessing on their marriage. In the marriage ceremony it says they accept God's blessing of children. They might just think children make their marriage perfect, so they are a blessing. Blessings are good things that are given to you.

Explain why some religious believers disagree with abortion. Use beliefs and teachings in your answer. (5)

Abortion goes against the Ten Commandments – do not kill. It is wrong as far as lots of religious people think because you are killing a baby, which has done nothing wrong, and which was made by God. So you are murdering God's creation. You will get punished after death for that. That baby's life is sacred, so it is wrong. But God forgives people, so if a woman had to have an abortion because her life was in danger, then it would be okay to have the abortion. Even religious people would agree then, because her life is sacred too.

A father should have the right to stop a woman having an abortion. Do you agree? Give reasons for your answer, showing you have thought about more than one point of view. Refer to religious arguments in your answer. (6)

This is right, because he made the baby too. She should discuss it with him and they should decide together. I think he should be able to make her have the baby – he can look after it when it is born if he wants it. They should only do the abortion if they both agree.

Exploring an exam question

A full exam question looks like this. It always has a stimulus, two AO2 evaluative questions, and two or three AO1 questions. The total is 18 marks, split equally between the two types of questions.

Look at the picture below. It shows a child.

On your exam paper, all the questions will have the same number of parts. So if the first is split into four parts, then all the rest will be too. If the first is split into five parts, all the rest will be too. In this book we have given you examples of each.

Just list them, don't bother writing lots out

Why did they want to have a child?

16 Give **three** reasons why couples choose to have a child. (3)

You might decide to give some secular reasons as well as religious ones – it will beef up your answer.
Stick to reasons for disagreeing; to describe reasons to agree just wastes time, because you can't get any marks for it

17 Abortion should be just the woman's decision.
   What do you think? Explain your opinion. (3)

18 Explain why many religious believers disagree with abortion. Refer to religious beliefs and teachings in your answer. (6)

19 A religious person should never have an abortion.
   Do you agree? Give reasons for your answer, showing you have thought about more than one point of view. Refer to religious arguments in your answer. (6)

Focus on whose right it is to decide; don't get sidetracked into whether abortion is OK or not

Remember to argue both sides and include religious arguments. The key word is 'never' so explore that – you might end up saying 'they should never, but sometimes they have to'

In her exam, Emma gave the following answers. Read them to try to work out what is good about her answers, and what could be done better, then try to write perfect answers for her. There are some pointers on page 93. You could use pages 6 and 7 to check the AO1/2 grids for how to answer parts **17**, **18** and **19** below.

16. They want to keep the family name going. They think a baby completes their family. They have a duty in their religion.

17. It is the doctor's decision not the woman's because the doctor can stop her. Other people should get a say – like the father, or their parents.

18. They believe it is murder, and the Ten Commandments say you can't murder. So Jews and Christians would say no to abortion. They also both think life is sacred, because God makes a child for you – like it is God's gift to you. If you abort it, you are throwing God's gift back in his face. When you have an abortion that is like saying that life isn't sacred at all – it is rubbish that you can throw away. The baby hasn't done anything either, so it is innocent but gets killed. But maybe the woman might die if she has the baby, like if she has cancer. Her life is sacred too, so it should be saved. Also if she has been raped, then it is awful to make her have the baby – it would make her go mad to remind her all the time.

19. When it says in the holy books don't kill, and abortion is killing a baby, I think they shouldn't have an abortion. For example, the Ten Commandments. Whenever you see protests outside abortion clinics, they are always religious people doing them, so they think it is wrong too. The Catholic Church says abortion is murder, and they say the baby is innocent so should never be made to suffer for what the parents have done. They say God knew the baby when it was inside its mother, showing how special it is. If you are a Catholic you would definitely not have an abortion, I think. I think if religious people want to be true to their religion, they have to follow the rules. They think a woman gets pregnant because God wants it, so if her life is in danger, it has to be up to God about that too.

Religion and early life: thought map

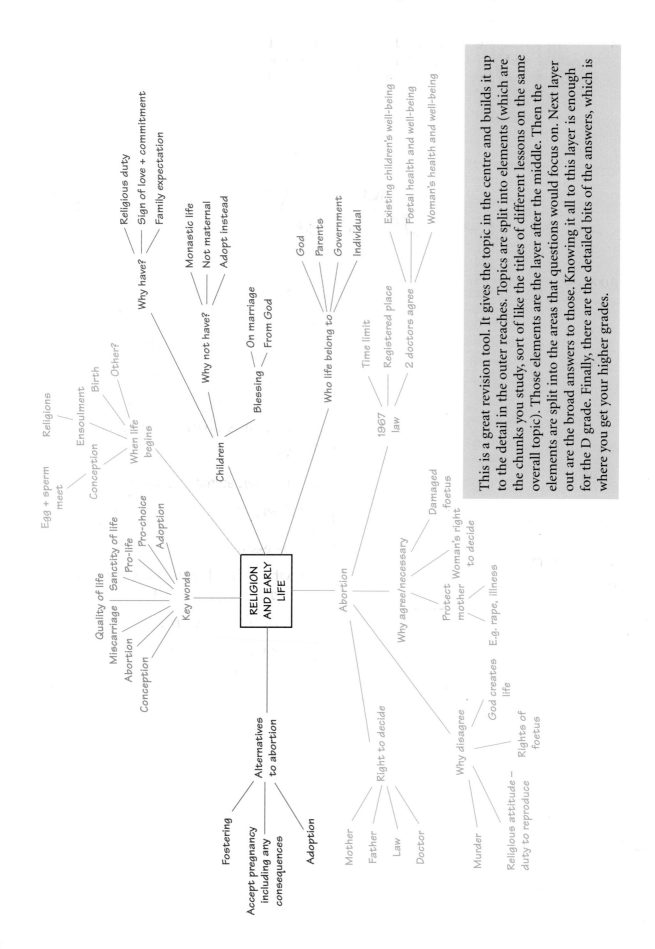

Egg + sperm meet — Religions

Conception — Ensoulment
Conception — Birth
Conception — Other?

When life begins

Miscarriage
Abortion — Pro-life
Conception — Pro-choice
Quality of life — Adoption
Sanctity of life

Key words

Religious duty
Sign of love + commitment
Family expectation

Why have?

Monastic life
Not maternal
Adopt instead

Why not have?

Blessing — On marriage
Blessing — From God

Children

God
Parents
Government
Individual

Who life belong to

Time limit
1967 law — Registered place
2 doctors agree

Existing children's well-being
Foetal health and well-being
Woman's health and well-being

RELIGION AND EARLY LIFE

Abortion

Damaged foetus
Why agree/necessary
Protect mother
Woman's right to decide
E.g. rape, illness

Why disagree
God creates life
Murder
Religious attitude – duty to reproduce
Rights of foetus

Mother
Father
Law
Doctor
Right to decide

Fostering
Accept pregnancy including any consequences
Adoption
Alternatives to abortion

This is a great revision tool. It gives the topic in the centre and builds it up to the detail in the outer reaches. Topics are split into elements (which are the chunks you study, sort of like the titles of different lessons on the same overall topic). Those elements are the layer after the middle. Then the elements are split into the areas that questions would focus on. Next layer out are the broad answers to those. Knowing it all to this layer is enough for the D grade. Finally, there are the detailed bits of the answers, which is where you get your higher grades.

Religion and early life: revision checklist

Go through the words and ideas on this page. They are the key ideas for this topic. For each word and each idea colour or mark it 'Know it' (green), 'Know a bit' (yellow), or 'Know little' (red). You then know which bits you have to spend most time on in your revision (the reds), and which ones are the easiest to remember but also the most tempting to revise again (green). This gives you a guide to focus and prioritise your revision.

Key words to learn ✔

Abortion

Adoption

Blessing

Conception

Fostering

Miracle of life

Pressure groups

Pro-Choice

Pro-Life

Quality of life

Rights

Sanctity of life

Viability

Subjects within topic – do you know? ✔

+ When life begins

+ Why children are a blessing

+ What we mean by miracle of life

+ What we mean by abortion

+ Why women have abortions

+ Arguments around the quality of life

+ The law about abortion

+ Religious attitudes to abortion

+ Examples where religious believers generally would accept an abortion is necessary

+ What rights all those involved have or should have – mother, father, foetus

+ Alternatives to abortion

+ The work of pressure groups on each side of the issue

Good luck on this topic!

Topic Five Religion, war and peace

Overview

For this topic you need to know about:

- religious attitudes to war
- the concepts of peace, justice and the sanctity of life and how they relate to the issues of war and peace
- the causes of war, including examples of recent wars
- why religious believers go to war including the criteria for a 'Just War' and 'Holy War'
- religious attitudes to peace and pacifism
- victims of war
- the work of organisations which help the victims of war
- the work of a religious believer who has worked for peace
- the role of peacekeeping forces such as the United Nations and NATO
- the issues related to terrorism, weapons of mass destruction (WMDs) and nuclear proliferation.

For each of these you need to be able to explain specific terms, give examples to show your understanding, explain why people may agree or disagree with the issues, write about problems associated with them, and give religious attitudes to them.

You also need to be able to evaluate (agree with and disagree with) statements about these issues.

Definitions of key terms

You could be asked to define any of these in the exam, or the phrases could be used in questions.

Holy War – fighting for a religious cause or God, found in Christian and Islamic teachings.

Just War – the rules of war which permit a religious person to fight, found in Christian and Sikh teachings.

Justice – to bring about what is right and fair for all people, correcting wrongs.

Nuclear proliferation – the increase in the number of countries that have nuclear weapons.

Pacifism – the belief that all violence is wrong.

Peace – the absence of war or conflict between groups or nations.

Peacekeeping forces – organisations that work in areas of conflict, to protect victims of war and establish and maintain peace between groups and nations.

Refugees – people who are forced to leave their homes and countries to find safety elsewhere.

Sanctity of life – the belief that life is special and sacred.

Terrorism – the use of threats and violence by groups to create a climate of fear to achieve their aims.

Victims of war – civilians who are affected by war.

War – two or more sides or nations involved in armed conflict.

Weapons of mass destruction (WMDs) – weapons that can kill large numbers of people and destroy vast areas of land.

Topic basics 1 – Key concepts about war

The first few parts in a full question on this topic are often to do
with some key concepts, and some generalised questions about war.
You need to be able to answer them – they are the easy marks.

Key concepts

Learn these terms.

Peace
- Is a virtue in all religions and means:
  - absence of war
  - harmony between people and nations
  - justice for all.

Justice
- What is right and fair.
- Respect for freedom.
- Just laws and punishment for offenders.
- Protection of individual and group rights.

Sanctity of life
- Refers to the idea that life is:
  - a gift of God
  - sacred and holy
  - valuable and precious
  - purposeful.

War

Types of war
- Between nations, e.g. First and Second World Wars, Vietnam War, Falklands War, Gulf War.
- Civil wars, e.g. former Yugoslavia, Sierra Leone, Rwanda.
- War against terrorism, e.g. Western allies against Al-Qaeda in specific countries, like Pakistan, and around the world.

Causes of war
- Defence against invader.
- Defence of religion, freedoms, way of life.
- Defence of a weaker nation.
- Pre-emptive strike to prevent expected attack.
- To gain land or resources.
- To remove an unjust leader.
- To end injustice, such as genocide.

How fought
- Conventional – using military personal and regular weapons.
- Weapons of mass destruction – nuclear, biological, chemical, radiological.

Effects of war
- Victims of war – killed, maimed, orphaned, refugees.
- Soldiers – killed, traumatised, desensitised.
- Environment – destruction of landscape, hazardous areas, e.g. landmines.
- Economy – loss of farming and industry, cost of rebuild.

Topic basics 2 – Just War, Holy War

Religious views

Just War theory

The Just War Theory is a set of rules which allows a religion to go to war. Both Christianity and Sikhism observe the Just War rules.

It is called 'Just' war because it comes from a sense of seeking justice, being fought with justice, and ending when justice is attained. These mean that war should fulfil all of the following rules:

- Be controlled by a just authority, e.g. an elected government.
- Have a just cause, e.g. it must not be for revenge.
- Have a clear aim to promote good over evil.
- Be a last resort – all diplomatic methods tried first.
- Be winnable – it is wrong to risk life if war cannot be won.
- Be conducted fairly – reasonable force used, civilians protected.
- Have a good outcome – benefits of war should outweigh the evil of war.
- The war ends when the aim is met.

Holy War

For Muslims a Holy War is the same as the Christian Just War. Believers have to fight as a duty. It is considered 'Holy' because it is sanctioned by Allah (God). The war must be fought keeping the following rules:

- Fought for God or faith.
- A last resort – enemy must have opportunity to make peace.
- Conducted fairly – just treatment of the enemy.
- For the protection of civilians and the landscape; certain buildings should be protected, for example religious buildings, and generally speaking towns should not be the battleground.
- For the restoration of justice and peace.
- The war ends when the aim is met.

This element in the exam is usually asking you for the rules which are followed. However, it could also ask you to name a war and show whether or not it fits with the rules.

Topic basics 3 – War in the modern world

What are WMDs?

Weapons of mass destruction – in other words a weapon which can kill many people (hundreds, if not thousands). Examples would be atomic and nuclear bombs.

The nuclear debate: should countries have nuclear weapons?

Reasons for proliferation (increase in nuclear countries):

- Nuclear weapons are seen as a deterrent which discourage attack and maintain peace – they could never be used.
- Disarmament agreements are easier to get because countries are equal in all having these WMDs.
- Use of WMDs made less likely, because the retaliation (with WMDs) would be so massive.

Reasons for disarmament (removal of nuclear weapons):

- Nuclear proliferation makes use of nuclear weapons more likely.
- No moral justification for their use, because their effect is indiscriminate, affecting civilians, land and buildings for many miles and for many years.
- Waste of valuable resources to produce them which could be used more effectively.
- Monetary cost of these weapons – their production and storage – could be used for peaceful means and for the benefit of humankind.
- Encourages other countries to develop them.

Religious attitudes to WMDs

- Use of WMDs, including nuclear weapons, is wrong because they have uncontrollable and extreme effects.
- WMDs are against Just War and Holy War theories.
- WMDs are against principles of peace, justice and sanctity of life.
- WMDs are used as a means of oppression so are wrong.
- Some believers accept the maintaining of a deterrent.

What is terrorism?

- Use of violence to create fear.
- Indiscriminate targeting of civilians and civilian areas.
- Non-democratic.
- Used to promote minority views, often fundamentalist.

Religious attitudes to terrorism

- Terrorism is against the principles of religious beliefs; it ignores justice, and leads to indiscriminate killing and harm.
- Religious teachings promote peace, justice and respect for life.
- A minority of fundamentalists use terrorist tactics.

Topic basics 4 – Responses to war and peace

Support for victims of war

Organisations that help victims e.g. Red Cross and Red Crescent Movement give:

- humanitarian aid, e.g. food, medical care, shelter, protection from attack
- support when conflict ends, e.g. rebuilding, locating lost family, care of orphans.

Peacekeeping forces

Organisations that work for peace, e.g. the United Nations or NATO:

- protect human rights in conflict zones
- use international pressure such as sanctions to end human rights abuses
- use military forces to implement peace agreements, monitor elections, conduct disarmament, etc.

Peace

Peace is the absence of war, and presence of harmony between peoples.

Religious views on peace
- Promoted by all religious faiths.
- The Golden Rule, e.g. 'treat people how you wish to be treated' is true in every religion.
- Necessary for people's physical and spiritual well-being.
- Some religious believers are pacifists.

Pacifists

Examples of pacifists include Quakers, Buddhists, the Dalai Lama and Martin Luther King Jr. Pacifists:

- Oppose all violence and war.
- Believe in the sanctity of life.
- Believe peace can be achieved using non-violent methods.
- Are often conscientious objectors who refuse to participate directly in fighting in wars on the grounds of conscience.

Individuals working for peace

Mohandas K. Gandhi (1869–1948)
- Hindu leader of India, campaigned for Indian independence from British rule in the 1930s and 1940s.
- Emphasised need for ahimsa (non-violence).
- Developed principle of satyagraha – resistance to oppression through non-violence.
- Led an organised campaign of civil disobedience to achieve his aims, e.g. the Salt March.

Dalai Lama (1935–)
- Spiritual leader of Tibetan Buddhists.
- Campaigns for Tibetan liberation from Chinese rule.
- Forced into exile from Tibet by the Chinese government.
- Believes all violence is wrong, peace is found in mutual respect.
- He has become an international symbol of peace.

Dietrich Bonhoeffer (1906–1945)
- Christian pacifist who founded the Confessing Church in Nazi-ruled Germany which spoke out against Nazi human rights abuses.
- Believed principles must be placed aside to overcome evil, even if this leads to personal suffering, hence his plot to assassinate Hitler, in spite of him being a pacifist, which led to his own execution.
- Helped Jews escape from death camps and worked to overthrow the Nazi Party.

Religious teachings: good specific teachings to learn

Buddhism

- The First Precept teaches not to harm others.
- 'Those who are free of resentful thoughts surely find peace' (Buddha).
- 'Hatred does not cease by hatred, hatred ceases by love' (Dhammapada).
- 'He should not kill a living being, nor cause it to be killed, nor should he incite another to kill' (Dhammapada).
- 'Peace can exist if everyone respects all others' (Dalai Lama).
- 'I will act towards others exactly as I would act towards myself' (Udana-varqa).

Sikhism

- 'As you value yourself, so value others, cause suffering to no one' (Guru Granth Sahib).
- 'When all else fails, it is right to draw the sword' (Guru Gobind Singh).
- 'His followers were to emerge as splendid warriors … having taken the baptism of the sword, would thence forward be firmly attached to the sword' (Guru Granth Sahib).
- 'The Lord is a haven of peace' (Adi Granth).
- 'Those who serve God find peace' (Guru Ram Das).
- 'Those who hate the one who has no hatred, according to the true justice of Dharma, they shall perish' (Guru Ram Das).

Islam

- 'Fight in the cause of Allah those who fight you, but do not transgress limits … if they cease let there be no hostility' (Qur'an).
- Lesser Jihad – to fight in the name of Allah and defend one's faith.
- 'Hate your enemy mildly, for he may become your friend one day' (Hadith).
- 'None of you truly believe until he wishes for his brothers what he wishes for himself' (Hadith).
- 'Fight them until there is no more oppression and there justice prevails' (Qur'an).
- 'Allah loves those who fight in his cause' (Qur'an).

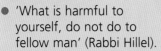

All religions teach: peace, justice, sanctity of life, the Golden Rule and charity

Judaism

- 'What is harmful to yourself, do not do to fellow man' (Rabbi Hillel).
- 'Get ready for war, call out your best warriors. Let your fighting men advance for the attack' (Ketuvim).
- 'It shall come to pass … nation shall not lift up sword against nation, neither shall they learn war anymore' (Nevi'im).
- 'If your enemy is hungry give him food to eat, if he is thirsty give him water to drink' (Proverbs).
- 'If they refuse to make peace and they engage you in battle, lay siege to that city' (Torah).
- 'By three things is the world preserved, on justice, on truth and on peace' (Rabbi Hillel).

Christianity

- 'Those who live by the sword die by the sword' (Jesus).
- 'Blessed are the peacemakers, for they shall inherit the earth' (Jesus).
- 'Love your neighbour' (Jesus).
- 'Treat others as you would like them to treat you' (Jesus).
- 'If someone slaps you on the right cheek, turn to him the other' (Jesus).
- 'Everyone must commit themselves to peace' (Pope John Paul II).

Hinduism

- 'An eye for an eye and the whole world will be blind' (Gandhi).
- 'I object to violence because the good it appears to do is only temporary, the evil is permanent' (Gandhi).
- 'The pursuit of truth does not permit violence being inflicted on one's opponent' (Gandhi).
- Ahimsa – the Hindu principle of non-violence to all living things.
- 'This is the sum of duty, do nothing to others which if done to you could cause pain' (Mahabharata).
- 'If you do not fight in this just war, you will neglect your duty, harm your reputation and commit the sin of omission' (Bhagavad Gita).

- Remember you only need to look at the religion(s) you have been taught.
- Remember to APPLY the teaching to the question after you have stated it – see page 4 for guidance on this.
- For most answers probably three specific teachings plus the generic ones will be sufficient.
- Notice some teachings can be used across more than one religion.

A useful revision technique: memory aids

Sometimes remembering stuff can be really tricky; you read notes through over and over and nothing seems to go in. One way to overcome this is to develop your own memory aids. The next two pages have some ideas for you to try and includes some useful examples. Remember the best memory aids are the ones you create for yourself – make them fun and personal and you will never forget them.

Pictograms

Visual images can be really useful ways to recall information. You can use labelled pictures, clip art or even your own drawings to create picture images to prompt your recall. The example here uses images of the key symbols used in a Christian infant baptism ceremony.

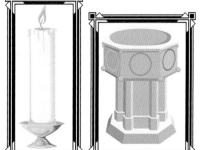

Kinaesthetics

In a nutshell this is getting physical with your revision. Kinaesthetics is a great way to remember quotes. Make up actions and do them as you say the quote, just like children learning the parts of the body in the song 'Heads, shoulders, knees and toes'. Here are three to try, the action to accompany each part of the quote is given in the brackets.

1. The body (run your hands up the sides of your body)
   Is a temple (put your hands together above your head making a triangle)
   Of the Holy Spirit (flap your hands out to the side like wings)
2. I (point at yourself)
   Knew (point at your head)
   You (point forwards as if someone is in front of you)
   Before you were born (Make a circular motion on your tummy)
3. Live by the sword (thrust your right arm upwards like brandishing a weapon)
   Die by the sword (thrust your right harm forward as though lunging with a sword).

Mnemonics and your RS revision

A mnemonic is simply a memory tool that helps you remember things like spellings, key points or sequences. They can be acronyms, invented words or rhymes. You might have used these before; do you recognise any of the ones below?

Acronyms
Acronyms are a phrase where the initial letter of each word triggers something else.

Richard Of York Gave Battle In Vain
This acronym is used to remember the sequence of colours in a rainbow.
Red Orange Yellow Green Blue Indigo Violet

Invented words
SOHCAHTOA
This is used in maths to remember how to work out the sine, cosine and tangent of an angle.

Rhymes
Thirty days hath September, April, June and November. All the rest have 31 excepting February alone, which has but 28 in fine, until a leap year makes it 29.

Use the mnemonic techniques to help you remember your RS. Here are some to get you started.

An acronym

Very Silly People Upset Innocent Souls

This acronym recalls the key causes of prejudice:

- Victim's experience
- Stereotyping
- Personal experience
- Upbringing
- Ignorance
- Scapegoating.

An invented word

CLOPJAW
This word uses initial letters to prompt recall of the key points in the Just War theory

- Controlled by authority
- Last resort
- Outcome is good
- Proportional force
- Just cause
- Aim achieved war ends
- Winnable.

A rhyme

'Life is a *valuable gift*
Far too *precious* to waste
Given by God for a *purpose*
So *holy and sacred* for us.'

This little rhyme helps to recall the key features in the religious teaching about the sanctity of life.

What questions on this topic look like

This page contains a range of examples of questions that could be on an exam paper for this topic. Practise them all to strengthen your knowledge and technique whilst revising. Page 73 has answers to some of these, with tips.

Check back to pages 6 and 7 to see the grids that examiners use to mark questions worth 3 marks or more, to help you answer them.

One-mark questions
● What is a pacifist?
● What is terrorism?

Two-mark questions
● Give two reasons why some countries go to war.
● Give two ways that people are affected by war.

Three-mark questions
● Describe the work of one individual who has worked for peace.
● Explain why many religious believers disagree with war.
● **Religious believers should be pacifists.** What do you think? Explain your opinion.

Four-mark questions
● Explain why some religious believers would not fight in a war.
● Describe the work of one organisation that helps the victims of war.
● Explain two reasons why many religious believers disagree with nuclear weapons.

Five-mark questions
● Explain religious teachings about Holy War.
● Explain using beliefs and teachings, religious attitudes to peace.
● Explain religious attitudes to the use of peacekeeping forces.

Six-mark questions
● Explain why some religious believers would fight in a war. Refer to beliefs and teachings in your answer.
● **Religious people should never take part in war**. Do you agree? Give reasons for your answer showing you have thought about more than one point of view. Refer to religious arguments in your answer.
● **Peace is impossible in the world**. Do you agree? Give reasons for your answer showing you have thought about more than one point of view. Refer to religious arguments in your answer.

Did you know an F-grade candidate will make barely any reference to religious teachings and beliefs and their answers will be of a superficial and general nature?

Did you know a C-grade candidate will include some teachings and beliefs in their answers, but these will mostly be general ideas that have been paraphrased and sometimes will not really fit the topic they are discussing?

Did you know an A-grade candidate will make very good use of teachings and beliefs, they will use specific references that exactly fit the topic they are discussing and paraphrases will be precise?

Which one are you? And how do you move to the next level?

Give two reasons why some countries go to war. (2)

1) For land.

2) To defend themselves against an attack.

Explain why many religious believers disagree with war. (3)

They say that too many innocent people die - wars are in towns, and bombs kill everyone. They also think we should try to solve problems peacefully, because violence leads to more violence later. It is against their beliefs to fight.

Explain why some religious believers would not fight in a war. (4)

They don't agree with why the war is happening, like the war in Iraq. They are pacifists – don't believe any wars solve anything. They don't want to kill people, who might be innocent. They think it has nothing to do with them, like if it was another country.

Explain religious teachings about Holy War. (5)

These were written hundreds of years ago in Hadith. Muslims follow them. The war has to follow these rules:

* *A just ruler tells them to fight.*
* *They have been attacked first.*
* *All men should fight, but only half of all the men in each place.*
* *Civilians must not be attacked or harassed.*
* *Prisoners of war must be well treated.*
* *War ends when the enemy asks for peace.*

Religious people should never take part in war. Do you agree? Give reasons for your answer showing you have thought about more than one point of view. Refer to religious arguments in your answer. (6)

I can see some reasons to agree – religious people should be peaceful. Jesus said peacemakers are blessed. You can't be a peacemaker if you are in a war. Also wars mean many innocent people killed, and all sorts of unnecessary damage. So they shouldn't fight.

On the other hand I can see reasons to disagree. If your country is attacked they need everybody to fight back. Saying 'Oh, I'm religious, I can't fight' won't keep you alive. You might end up more likely dead – say if the ones who attacked hated your religion. Plus sometimes the war is for an important reason, like to stop the people in another country being killed for no reason – like in the Second World War. Even religious people have to fight against evil like that to stop it – God would want them to. Finally, the religions have rules for wars, so it must be okay for religious people to fight a war.

Exploring an exam question

A full exam question looks like this. It always has a stimulus, two AO2 evaluative questions, and two or three AO1 questions. Total is 18 marks, split equally between the two types of questions.

Look at the picture below. It shows a UN Peacekeeping Forces soldier.

On your exam paper, all the questions will have the same number of parts. So if the first is split into four parts, then all the rest will be too. If the first is split into five parts, all the rest will be too. In this book we have given you examples of each.

The photo and its title give you one to write about

Think about if this should always be the case, or when it is impossible so that you expand your answer

21 Describe the work of one organisation that works for peace. (3)

22 **Religious believers should be pacifists.** What do you think? Explain your opinion. (3)

This is asking you to give an example of a war and show how it fits the Just War rules

Just give two reasons, don't bother explaining

23 Give two reasons why countries might go to war. (2)

24 Explain what some religious people believe is a Just War. (4)

25 **It is wrong for countries to have nuclear weapons.** Do you agree? Give reasons for your answer showing that you have thought about more than one point of view. Refer to religious arguments in your answer. (6)

You have to argue both sides, and give religious arguments to get full marks. Don't forget to explain every point you make

James gave the following answers. Read them to try to work out what is good about his answers, and what could be done better, then try to write perfect answers for him. There are some pointers on page 93. You could use pages 6 and 7 to check the AO1/2 grids for how to answer parts **22, 23** and **24** below.

21. The United Nations is the biggest peacekeeping force in the world. Their soldiers are from all countries and wear blue berets. They go to war zones to try to make sure that innocent people are not killed. The UN also works with the leaders of countries who are at war to help them make peace agreements and sort out their differences. They then help the countries by providing them with funds and resources to rebuild after a war has ended.

22. I don't think religious believers should be pacifists everyone should be ready to fight for their country if they are needed, or a lot of innocent people would die. Also being a pacifist could be seen as wrong in Sikhism because you should be prepared to fight for your beliefs and defend people against injustice and tyranny, this is what Guru Gobind Singh said when he formed the Khalsa.

23. To stop an invader and in self-defence.

24. Sikhs say that a war is OK to fight if it is a last resort. They may have tried to make peace, but the enemy won't. They should also fight if it is a just cause such as to defend your religion or protect innocent people. The war must never be for revenge or fought with hatred because this can lead to terrible things happening like murdering civilians. A Sikh soldier should always fight with honour and the war must end when its aims have been met.

25. Some people would agree with this because nuclear weapons are weapons of mass destruction, they are so dangerous that they could never actually be used. This means that they are actually a waste of money because countries spend millions of pounds on something that is never going to be used. Sikhs would agree with this because they believe that the world was created by God. If nuclear weapons were used it would destroy God's planet. They also think that the money could be used in much better ways such as helping the poor. Not everyone would agree with this because we have had nuclear weapons for a long time and they have helped to bring about peace between countries like America and Russia. Some people think that nuclear weapons could be used in a controlled way if needed, they were used in Japan and that didn't bring an end to the world but it did end the war.

Religion, war and peace: thought map

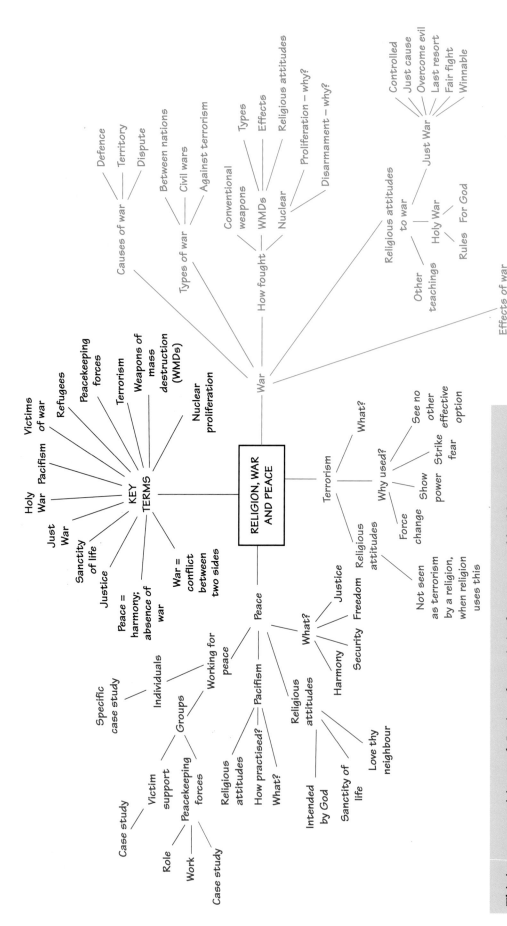

This is a great revision tool. It gives the topic in the centre and builds it up to the detail in the outer reaches. Topics are split into elements (which are the chunks you study, sort of like the titles of different lessons on the same overall topic). Those elements are the layer after the middle. Then the elements are split into the areas that questions would focus on. Next layer out are the broad answers to those. Knowing it all to this layer is enough for the D grade. Finally, there are the detailed bits of the answers, which is where you get your higher grades.

Religion, war and peace: revision checklist

Go through the words and ideas on this page. They are the key ideas for this topic. For each word and each idea colour or mark it 'Know it' (**green**), 'Know a bit' (yellow), or 'Know little' (**red**). You then know which bits you have to spend most time on in your revision (the **reds**), and which ones are the easiest to remember but also the most tempting to revise again (**green**). This gives you a guide to focus and prioritise your revision.

Key words to learn ✔

Holy War

Justice

Just War

Nuclear proliferation

Pacifism

Peace

Peacekeeping forces

Refugees

Sanctity of life

Terrorism

Victims of war

War

Weapons of mass destruction (WMDs)

Subjects within topic – do you know? ✔

✦ Religious attitudes to peace and justice

✦ Why many religious believers believe in pacifism

✦ How the sanctity of life can be used to argue for and against war

✦ What war is

✦ Why war happens

✦ Examples of recent wars

✦ Why religious believers might go to war

✦ Attitudes of religious believers to war

✦ Explanation of Just War, including its rules and examples of wars

✦ Explanation of Holy War, including its rules and examples of wars

✦ The effects of war on people including how people can be maimed and made refugees

✦ The work of an organisation that helps the victims of wars

✦ The role of peacekeeping forces and how they may carry this out

✦ The work of a named religious believer who has worked for peace, and how faith influenced them to do this

✦ Religious attitudes to terrorism

✦ Religious attitudes to weapons of mass destruction (WMDs)

✦ Religious attitudes to nuclear proliferation

 Good luck on this topic!

Topic Six Religion and young people

Overview

For this topic you need to know about:

- birth and initiation ceremonies in one religious tradition
- the role of the home, upbringing, spirituality, moral codes and religious beliefs as an influence on decision making and life choices
- examples of activities organised by faith groups for young people, their purpose and contribution to the lives of young people
- commitment and membership of faith groups including coming of age ceremonies
- rights and responsibilities of young people including freedom of choice, relationships and rules
- problems and benefits for young people of commitment to faith
- role of schools including RS, assemblies and faith schools.

For each of these you need to be able to explain specific terms, give examples to show your understanding, explain why people may agree or disagree with the issues, write about problems associated with them, and give religious attitudes to them.

You also need to be able to evaluate (agree with and disagree with) statements about these issues.

Definitions of key terms

You could be asked to define any of these in the exam, or the phrases could be used in questions.

Assemblies – occasions where students are brought together in schools for collective worship.

Birth ceremonies – religious rituals that are performed either when a child is born or in early infancy.

Brotherhood – support derived by being part of a community with shared values, aspirations, etc. (sisterhood is the female form of this).

Coming of age ceremonies – religious rituals performed to celebrate a child's move to adulthood within a faith; these can also be initiation ceremonies in some faiths.

Empowerment – developing confidence in individuals or groups.

Faith schools – schools which are supported by a specific faith group; the school ethos and curriculum reflect the beliefs of that faith.

Generation gap – a difference between the views of young people and their elders.

Initiation ceremonies – religious rituals performed to formally enter a person into a faith.

Marginalisation – the social process of becoming isolated and left out; can affect individuals and groups.

Moral codes – rules about morality which influence the way people live their lives.

Peer pressure – the influence of friends on each other.

Responsibilities – duties that a person has to others, their faith, etc.

Rights – entitlements that all people should have.

Secular society – all aspects of society that are not connected with or influenced by religion.

Spirituality – a sense of awe and wonder, something outside of everyday human experience.

Topic basics 1 – Birth and commitment ceremonies

Birth ceremonies

Buddhism

- no specific religious ceremonies, but have cultural ones
- monk may visit home to bless child and chants scriptures as a blessing
- gifts given to sangha by parents
- parents may visit temple and make offerings
- some Buddhists have the child named at a temple
- water is sprinkled on child, symbolising cleanliness.

Christianity

- infant baptism in many Christian denominations
- ceremony welcomes the child into the Christian faith
- baby dressed in white to symbolise purity
- priest asks parents and godparents three questions about their faith
- water is taken from font and sprinkled on baby's forehead three times
- priest says, 'In the name of the father, son and holy spirit'
- symbol of cross made and child's name announced
- a lighted candle is given to parents as symbol of Jesus (light in the world).

Hinduism

- Hindu ceremonies are called samskaras
- some take place before birth, the rest are after birth
- jatakarma takes place soon after birth:
  - the father makes the aum symbol on the baby's tongue with mixture of ghee and honey, symbolising hope for the child to have sweet nature
  - the father also whispers the name of the Ultimate Reality into the baby's ear to welcome him or her into the faith
- namakarana takes place ten to twelve days after birth:
  - the baby is dressed in new clothes and taken to the temple
  - an astrologer reads out the child's horoscope
  - the child's name is announced
  - the family make a havan (fire sacrifice) and make offerings to deities.

Birth ceremonies *(continued)*

Islam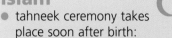

- tahneek ceremony takes place soon after birth:
  - the father whispers the Adhan (call to prayer) in child's right ear
  - the father whispers the Iqamah (call to prayer before salat) into left ear
  - the child is now welcomed into faith
  - a date is placed on the child's tongue, symbolising hope for sweet nature
- aqiqah ceremony takes place shortly afterwards:
  - the head is shaved, hair weighed and family make equivalent donation of money – this purifies the child
  - verses from the Qur'an are read aloud
  - the child's name is announced and the Adhan again is whispered into child's ear
  - male children are circumcised
  - the family pay for an animal to be sacrificed and its meat given to the poor.

Judaism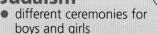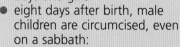

- different ceremonies for boys and girls
- eight days after birth, male children are circumcised, even on a sabbath:
  - a mohel carries out the circumcision procedure
  - the child held by honoured guest called a Sandek
  - the father reads blessing from the Torah
  - the mohel blesses child and announces his name
  - the mother feeds the child and celebrations are held
- female children's names are announced in a synagogue at the first sabbath after birth
- some Jews have a zeved habat ceremony for girls:
  - the rabbi blesses the child in the home
  - celebrations follow.

Sikhism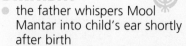

- the father whispers Mool Mantar into child's ear shortly after birth
- honey placed on the child's tongue, symbolising hope for a sweet future
- a naming ceremony takes place in gurdwara soon after birth:
  - the parents take ingredients for Karah Parshad, and a romalla as gifts
  - readings from the Guru Granth Sahib
  - granthi stirs amrit (sugar water) with kirpan
  - drops of amrit placed on child's tongue, prayers for long life and sweet nature
  - granthi then opens Guru Granth Sahib at a random page
  - the first letter of the first word on left-hand page is the initial for the child's name
  - the parents choose the name, Granthi announces this to the congregation
  - Karah Parshad shared by congregation, parents make donation to charity.

Ceremonies of commitment

Buddhism

- no specific ceremony to become a Buddhist
- some choose to recite the Three Refuges to mark acceptance of Buddhist way of life
- Theravada Buddhists have a ceremony to enter a monastery:
  - the novice must be free from debt and know the passages to recite at the ceremony
  - before the ceremony he will visit the wat (monastery), make offerings and ring a gong
  - day before the ceremony he walks in procession wearing white with his head shaved – these are symbols of purity
  - on his initiation day he circles the wat four times in rich clothing carrying incense, a candle and a lotus flower
  - he removes rich clothing and throws coins on floor – this symbolises leaving worldly life behind, like Siddartha Gotama (the Buddha)
  - he enters the ordination hall and asks to be admitted
  - the abbot asks him questions and he must answer in Pali
  - finally, he dons yellow robes and begins life as monk.

Christianity

- confirmation ceremony at around twelve years of age confirms the promises made for the young person at Baptism:
  - the young person attends preparation classes
  - the service is conducted by a bishop
  - he asks candidates the three questions asked at birth, they respond yes
  - he lays hands on their forehead and confirms their commitment to the Church
  - Holy Communion is then celebrated, and confirmation candidates take first communion
- the Baptist Church has a believer's baptism:
  - candidates make confession of sins and acceptance of Christ as saviour
  - the minister leads them into the baptistery, they are fully immersed under the water
  - symbolises dying to sin and rising to life again in Christ.

Hinduism

- sacred thread ceremony for boys at around twelve years symbolises full entry into their caste:
  - takes place in a garden around a sacred fire
  - puja (worship) conducted by the boy's teacher
  - sacred thread presented to him, placed over his left shoulder across his body to the right hip
  - the boy is now allowed to conduct religious ceremonies, recite scripture and marry.

Ceremonies of commitment *(continued)*

Islam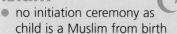

- no initiation ceremony as child is a Muslim from birth
- at the age of four, children take part in a Bismillah ceremony:
  - remembers Prophet Muhammad (pbuh) receiving the revelations from angel Jibrail
  - the child learns the Bismillah passage from the Qur'an
  - at the ceremony they recite the passage to family and friends
  - gifts received and celebration follow – it marks the beginning of their religious education
- children take on further religious duties as they grow up.

Judaism

- at the age of thirteen there is the Bar Mitzvah ceremony for boys, Bat Mitzvah for girls aged twelve. The title means 'Son of the Commandments' ('Daughter' for girls). The ceremony symbolises moving from childhood to adulthood:
  - period of training and preparation with a rabbi before the ceremony
  - ceremony takes place in synagogue on the Sabbath nearest boy's thirteenth birthday
  - Torah scrolls prepared at the bimah by the rabbi
  - the boy is then invited to come and read passages in Hebrew
  - sermon then given by the rabbi and the boy is blessed
  - the boy is now obligated to keep all of the commandments
  - celebrations follow.

Sikhism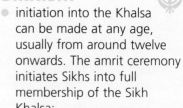

- initiation into the Khalsa can be made at any age, usually from around twelve onwards. The amrit ceremony initiates Sikhs into full membership of the Sikh Khalsa:
  - the ceremony is conducted in front of the Guru Granth Sahib with five Khalsa Sikhs dressed to represent the Panj Piare
  - amrit is stirred with a khanda – a double-edged sword
  - the granthi recites passages from the Guru Granth Sahib and one of the khalsa members recites the vows the initiates must promise to keep
  - the initiates kneel on one knee showing readiness to defend faith
  - amrit is sprinkled on their hair and eyes
  - each person drinks some of the amrit from same bowl, showing equality
  - prayers and hymns follow, the ceremony ends with sharing of Karah Parshad
  - men take the name Singh (meaning lion), women Kaur (meaning princess).

Topic basics 2 – Young people and religion

How young people make moral choices

- Upbringing – including parents, other family, environment.
- Spirituality – inner personal conscience and awareness.
- Moral codes – the law, family values, religious teachings, personal values.
- Religious beliefs – influence on development, choice to maintain faith.
- Peer pressure – need to fit in with group, conform to accepted norms of group.
- Other influences – education, the law, culture, media.

Being religious

- Faith groups – activities for young people.
- Worship – youth services, ceremonies for birth and commitment, religious instruction.
- Festivals – fun for children, stories, celebrations, gifts.
- Youth organisations – Scout and Guide Movement, Boys and Girls Brigades.
- Religious holidays – Taize, retreats, community sponsored breaks.
- Social activities – youth clubs, sport and recreation, prayer groups.
- Voluntary work – gap-year activities, sponsored events, participation in community.

Benefits for young believers
- Range of activities.
- Membership and belonging.
- Sense of meaning and purpose.
- Empowerment.
- Support of brotherhood/sisterhood.

Problems for young believers
- Secular society – conflicts such as dress and popular culture.
- Marginalisation – social process of exclusion and being left out.
- Peer pressure – lack of acceptance of faith and misunderstanding.
- Discrimination – religious prejudice leading to discrimination.
- Generation gap – conflict between young people and their elders due to misunderstanding, contrasting values, etc.

Rights and responsibilities

Rights are the things we are entitled to, such as an education, protection under law, healthcare, welfare support and so on. However, we can only expect to have rights if we take responsibility for them. With rights come responsibilities. So we uphold the law, and obey it in order to be protected by it. Young people's rights are enshrined in UK law, and the Declaration of the Rights of the Child.

Freedom of choice

This is the idea that we have a choice in our decisions and actions. However:

- There are always limitations, e.g. the law, age, parental restrictions, religious obligations.
- The generation gap can lead to conflict between young people and older members of society.
- Religions impose rules on people with the need to obey for the sake of their own soul, even though they all mention free will.
- Peer groups impose rules on us by expecting us to behave in certain ways.
- Our various relationships influence us and shape our use of freedom of choice.

Role of schools

State schools
- Religious studies.
- Assemblies (collective worship).

Faith schools
- Differences to state schools, e.g. admissions rules based on the faith of the students' families.
- Reasons for faith schools, e.g. to educate within the context of Catholic belief, so that all aspects of the school follow Catholic ethos.
- Reasons against faith schools, e.g. they can be thought to promote bigotry as they instil the named faith into all students regardless of their own faith.

Religious teachings: good specific teachings to learn

Christianity ✝

- Spare the rod, spoil the child (Proverbs 13:24).
- Suffer the little children to come unto me, and forbid them not: for of such is the kingdom of God (Mark 10:14).
- Run from anything that gives you the evil thoughts that young men often have, but stay close to anything that makes you want to do right (II Timothy 2:22).
- Don't let anyone look down on you because you are young, but set an example for the believers in speech, in life, in love, in faith and in purity (I Timothy 4:12).
- Children, obey your parents in everything, for this pleases the Lord (Colossians 3:20).

Islam ☪

- Be good to your parents (Qur'an 6:151).
- The Prophet Muhammad (pbuh) said that paradise lies at the feet of your mother (Hadith).
- Those who show the most perfect faith are kindest to their families (Hadith).
- When asked which acts were most good, the Prophet replied first prayer and second duty to parents (Hadith).
- The Prophet warned that those who did not care for their parents would not enter paradise (Hadith).

Buddhism ☸

- In the Rahula Sutta the Buddha instructs his son of the importance of learning from his mistakes.
- 'Neither fire nor wind, birth nor death can erase our good deeds' (Buddha).
- 'We are what we think. All that we are arises with our thoughts. With our thoughts, we make our world' (Buddha).
- 'Morality, compassion, decency, wisdom, these qualities must be taught through moral education in a social environment, so that a more humane world may emerge' (Dalai Lama).
- 'Teaching our children the dharma is the best way to safeguard their minds and hearts from the many unwholesome and negative influences of our modern society' (Buddhist Faith Fellowship).

All religions teach: importance of family, belonging, respect for parents and equality

Judaism ✡

- Honour your father and mother (Exodus 20:12).
- Don't let the excitement of being young cause you to forget about your Creator: Honour Him in your youth (Ecclesiastes 12:1).
- Do not withhold correction from a child, beat him with a rod and deliver his soul from hell (Proverbs 23:13–14).
- Listen, my son, to your father's instruction and do not forsake your mother's teaching (Proverbs 1:8).
- When my father and my mother forsake me, then the Lord will take me up (Psalm 27:10).

Hinduism ॐ

- A man in this world without learning, is like a beast of the field (Hindu proverb).
- Action is greater than inaction. Perform your task in life (Bhagavad Gita).
- The evil deeds of those who destroy the family tradition and give rise to unwanted children, destroy community projects and family welfare. (Bhagavad Gita).
- Ganesha is particularly important for young people as he is the God of intelligence.

Sikhism ☬

- Gazing upon the tiny bodies of your children, love has welled up within your heart; you are proud of them (Guru Granth Sahib).
- the faithful uplift and redeem their family and relations (Guru Granth Sahib).
- Duty to the One Lord is upon the heads of all (Guru Granth Sahib).
- You are born and you come out, and your mother and father are delighted to see your face (Guru Granth Sahib).

- Remember you only need to look at the religion(s) you have been taught.
- Remember to APPLY the teaching to the question after you have stated it – see page 4 for guidance on this.
- For most answers probably three specific teaching(s) plus the generic ones will be sufficient.
- Notice some teachings can be used across more than one religion.

A useful revision technique: postcards

Revision postcards are a really good way to summarise your notes. They are also portable, so you can take your revision with you and make the most of those moments when you are on the bus or waiting for an appointment. Make them to fit in your blazer pocket and you can always have something purposeful to do in those odd moments.

The following examples show some of the different types of information you can put on your postcards. For maximum effect, stick to the main themes of a topic and don't be tempted to overload the postcard with too much information. If you team up with some of your classmates you can make and exchange postcards, and share the revision between you.

Why young people join faith groups
- Expectations of parents
- For the activities which they enjoy
- Their own sense of spirituality
- Peer group/school expectation
- For companionship

Christian and Buddhist birth ceremonies

Christian	Buddhist
At church	No official religious ceremonies in Buddhism. Parents take child to temple
Baby dressed in white for purity	Monk blesses child
Questions to godparents about bringing the child up in the faith	Monk recites some verses of scripture
Sign of cross on baby's forehead, with blessing	Monk splashes water on baby's head – cleanness and protection from evil
Water poured over baby's head three times – Trinity	Parents give offerings of food, money, incense, flowers to show thanks
Candle given to parents – Jesus is light of world	

Why schools do RS
- Help young people understand the society they live in
- Encourage tolerance and acceptance
- To explore important issues in society
- To explore the idea of spirituality
- To encourage young people to show empathy for others

Activities of faith groups for young people
- Worship – youth services, ceremonies for birth and commitment, religious instruction
- Festivals – fun for children, stories, celebrations, gifts
- Youth organisations – Scout and Guide Movement, Boys and Girls Brigades
- Religious holidays – Taize, retreats, community sponsored breaks
- Social activities – youth clubs, sport and recreation, prayer groups
- Voluntary work – gap-year activities, sponsored events, participation in community

What questions on this topic look like

This page contains a range of examples of questions that could be on an exam paper for this topic. Practise them all to strengthen your knowledge and technique while revising. Page 87 has answers to some of these, with tips.

Check back to pages 6 and 7 to see the grids that examiners use to mark questions worth three marks or more, to help you answer them.

One-mark questions
- Give one advantage of schools having an assembly.
- What is a moral code?

Two-mark questions
- Give two different influences on young people as they grow up.
- Briefly explain what is meant by the generation gap.

Three-mark questions
- Describe an initiation ceremony in one religion you have studied.
- Explain why a young person may be a member of a faith group.
- **Faith schools are the best choice for children from religious families**. What do you think? Explain your opinion.

Four-mark questions
- Explain the rights and responsibilities of young people in a faith group.
- Describe some of the ways that faith groups can encourage young people to join.
- Explain two reasons why some parents choose to send their children to a faith school.

Five-mark questions
- Explain the birth ceremonies in one religion you have studied.
- Explain how the influences on young people can affect their life choices.
- Explain the advantages and disadvantages for young people who have religious faith.

Six-mark questions
- Explain the role of schools in contributing to young people's understanding of religious beliefs.
- **Parents should not make their children follow a specific religion**. Do you agree? Give reasons for your answer showing that you have thought about more than one point of view. Refer to religious arguments in your answer.
- **Religion is too old fashioned for young people today**. Do you agree? Give reasons for your answer showing that you have thought about more than one point of view. Refer to religious arguments in your answer.

Did you know an F-grade candidate will rarely write in a way that makes clear what they mean? Their answers may be brief and often not actually answering the question that they have been asked.

Did you know that a C-grade candidate often knows and understands a lot of their course material? However, they do not use this well in their answers, often repeating points or not focusing on the specifics of the question asked. Their answers can be overlong and they sometimes run out of time and do not complete all the questions.

Did you know that an A-grade candidate writes clear and precise answers to the questions asked? They structure their responses clearly and avoid repetition of points; they will time their answers to allow them to read through and check before the end of the exam.

So, which are you?

Briefly explain what is meant by the generation gap. (2)

The generation gap is young and old people not understanding each other, e.g. old people think young people listen to rubbish music.

Faith schools are the best choice for children from religious families. What do you think? Explain your opinion. (3)

I agree with this because I am a Muslim and my parents think that it is important for me to be able to practise my faith whilst I am at school. A Muslim school provides opportunities for prayer and has facilities for wudu which is important because some of the prayer times are during the school day. As well as studying the usual subjects I also get to do lessons on the Qu'ran which is the Muslim holy book.

Explain the rights and responsibilities of young people in a faith group. (4)

Young people have lots of rights; they have a right to an education; a loving home; and to be nurtured and cared for. As they get older they also have responsibilities to become active members of the community and law-abiding citizens. They shouldn't be made to be religious if they don't want to be.

Explain the birth ceremonies in one religion you have studied. (5)

In Christianity when a baby is born they have a baptism ceremony. This takes place in a church, usually on a Sunday. The baby is dressed in white and the parents will ask two friends to be the baby's godparents, they might ask more if they want to. At the church the vicar holds the baby and he pours water on their head and blesses them. Then he says the baby's name and the godparents hold a candle. After they have done the church service there is usually a big party and people give the baby presents like silver jewellery.

Religion is too old fashioned for young people today. Do you agree? Give reasons for your answer showing that you have thought about more than one point of view. Refer to religious arguments in your answer. (6)

I agree with this statement. Religion is old fashioned you can see that because most people who go to church are old. When you do go to a church they have really old fashioned music and sing boring hymns. Religion is also out of date, it says stuff like the world was created by God but science has shown that it was created by a big bang. A lot of religious ideas are also wrong today, like they say you shouldn't have sex before marriage and being gay is bad, which I don't agree with and neither do lots of my friends. The Bible was written so long ago that it just doesn't have anything to say about lots of things that are important today like cloning and the environment. If someone young is in a religion it's only because they are made to do it by their parents, so yes I think religion is old fashioned.

Tip

Sometimes terms can be hard to explain; using an example can help to demonstrate that you do understand the term. Two marks awarded here.

Tip

This candidate has written a full personal response to the evaluation question. This is permitted because the three-mark questions ask for your opinion. The candidate backs her opinion up with reasons and evidence. Full marks awarded.

Tip

The candidate has stated some rights and responsibilities of young people, but has not explained what these mean or why they are important. They have also missed the focus of the question. The examples they use are of a general nature, rather than specifically about being in a faith group. Two marks awarded as some of their ideas could relate to being in a faith group.

Tip

It is really important to know what the command words in the question mean so that you can target your answer. This candidate has described some of the main elements of a baptism service well, however the command word was to 'explain' what happens. They will get some credit for their knowledge but, without explanation of some of the things they refer to they will receive no more than two marks.

Tip

This candidate makes some good points that are relevant to the question asked. Unfortunately they only refer to one side of the argument and so even though they do have several reasons here they will not achieve more than three marks.

Exploring an exam question

A full exam question looks like this. It always has a stimulus, two AO2 evaluative questions, and two or three AO1 questions. Total is 18 marks, split equally between the two types of questions.

Look at the statements below.

On your exam paper, all the questions will have the same number of parts. So if the first is split into four parts, then all the rest will be too. If the first is split into five parts, all the rest will be too. In this book we have given you examples of each.

Living here is boring, there is nothing for young people to do

Young people today don't know what music is, they just listen to noise

Only a simple definition is required

26 What is meant by the generation gap? (1)

Don't forget – it is easier to get full marks on these by arguing from both sides – one reason and a bit of explanation on each side should do it

27 Describe the activities faith groups provide for young people. (4)

Make a list and explain them a little

28 Religious studies should not be taught in schools. What do you think? Explain your opinion. (3)

It wants to know why they have ceremonies, not what happens at them

29 Explain why some religious people have ceremonies when a baby is born. (4)

30 Parents should not influence the religious beliefs of their children. Do you agree? Give reasons for your answer showing that you have thought about more than one point of view. Refer to religious arguments in your answer.

Explore why and how they do in your answer to this

Bethany gave the following answers. Read them to try to work out what is good about her answers, and what could be done better, then try to write perfect answers for her. There are some pointers on page 93. You could use pages 6 and 7 to check the AO1/2 grids for how to answer parts 27, 28 and 29 below.

26. It's when old people think young people are noisy.

27. Some churches organise events for young people like discos, youth clubs and Sunday school for little kids. They also have things like Christmas and Harvest festivals which children go to.

28. I don't agree with this I really like my RS lessons, they have been good fun. We have lots of debates and watch lots of videos. RS has helped me to understand about other people's beliefs and I think this is a good thing.

29. Christians have a christening when a baby is born. They do this to name the baby and to thank God for their child and to make them a Christian. Having this ceremony is also a good time to introduce the baby to all the family as there is usually a party afterwards.

30. I don't agree with this because parents should teach their children about their religion – it is one of their jobs as a parent. This helps the children to know who they are and about their religion. In the Bible it says that parents should teach their children and there is a quote about Jesus saying that children should be allowed to come to him. People who would disagree with me would say that kids should make up their own minds, but they can't do this until they are older. How would they know what to decide if they hadn't been taught about their religion when they were young?

Religion and young people: thought map

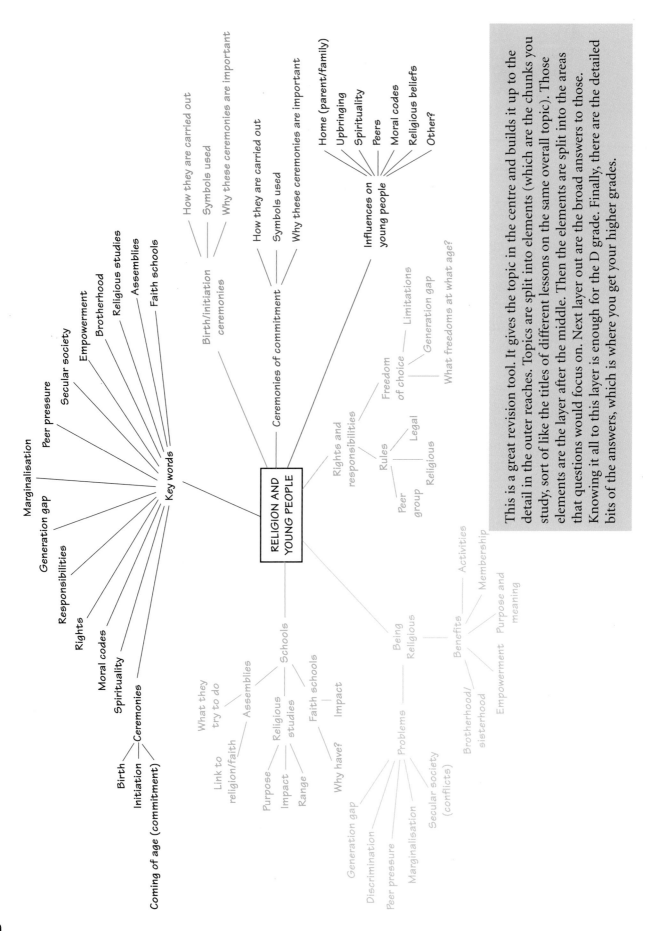

Key words

- Marginalisation
- Peer pressure
- Generation gap
- Secular society
- Responsibilities
- Empowerment
- Rights
- Brotherhood
- Moral codes
- Religious studies
- Spirituality
- Assemblies
- Ceremonies
- Faith schools
- Initiation
- Birth
- Coming of age (commitment)

Birth/Initiation ceremonies
- How they are carried out
- Symbols used
- Why these ceremonies are important

Ceremonies of commitment
- How they are carried out
- Symbols used
- Why these ceremonies are important

Influences on young people
- Home (parent/family)
- Upbringing
- Spirituality
- Peers
- Moral codes
- Religious beliefs
- Other?

RELIGION AND YOUNG PEOPLE

Rights and responsibilities
- Freedom of choice
  - Limitations
  - Generation gap
- Rules
  - Legal
  - Religious
  - Peer group
- What freedoms at what age?

Schools
- Assemblies
  - What they try to do
  - Link to religion/faith
- Religious studies
  - Purpose
  - Impact
  - Range
- Faith schools
  - Impact
  - Why have?

Being Religious
- Problems
  - Generation gap
  - Discrimination
  - Peer pressure
  - Marginalisation
  - Secular society (conflicts)
  - Brotherhood/sisterhood
- Benefits
  - Activities
  - Membership
  - Purpose and meaning
  - Empowerment

This is a great revision tool. It gives the topic in the centre and builds it up to the detail in the outer reaches. Topics are split into elements (which are the chunks you study, sort of like the titles of different lessons on the same overall topic). Those elements are the layer after the middle. Then the elements are split into the areas that questions would focus on. Next layer out are the broad answers to those. Knowing it all to this layer is enough for the D grade. Finally, there are the detailed bits of the answers, which is where you get your higher grades.

Religion and young people: revision checklist

Go through the words and ideas on this page. They are the key ideas for this topic. For each word and each idea colour or mark it 'Know it' (green), 'Know a bit' (yellow), or 'Know little' (red). You then know which bits you have to spend most time on in your revision (the reds), and which ones are the easiest to remember but also the most tempting to revise again (green). This gives you a guide to focus and prioritise your revision.

Key words to learn ✔

Assemblies

Birth ceremony

Brotherhood

Coming of age ceremony

Empowerment

Faith schools

Generation gap

Initiation ceremony

Marginalisation

Moral codes

Peer pressure

Responsibilities

Rights

Secular society

Spirituality

Subjects within topic – do you know? ✔

✦ Birth ceremonies for the religions you are studying – descriptions of the rituals and their meaning

✦ Initiation/coming of age ceremonies for the religions you are studying – descriptions of the rituals and their meaning

✦ How young people are influenced by their parents, upbringing, spirituality, beliefs and moral codes

✦ Why young people belong to faith groups

✦ Activities involved in being part of a faith group

✦ What is helpful about belonging to a faith group

✦ Religious views on the rights and responsibilities of young people

✦ Religious views on freedom of choice, relationships and rules

✦ The problems faced by young people with faith including the generation gap, marginalisation, peer pressure and living in a secular society

✦ How having faith helps young people – including ideas of empowerment, purpose, brotherhood

✦ How schools present and support religion and young people's beliefs including through RS, assemblies and faith schools

Good luck on this topic!

Pointers for sample answers to exam questions

Pointers for Dewi's answers on page 19

01 Dewi does what he has to – two correct reasons given. Full marks.

02 Does he really help us understand the term? And do humans really want animals to have the same rights? Don't think so for either. No marks here.

03 He writes about two religions – a good tactic as it shows wider knowledge. He gives relevant ideas for each religion too. Is he really telling us about attitudes to animal rights though? Perhaps he is just telling us about attitudes to animals – so he is going to miss out on the top level(s). Three marks.

04 Only one-sided, but for a three-marker, that is ok. No religious content either. The answer is more about whether bull-fighting is okay or not, rather than whether religious people should try to get it banned. Bull-fighting is about killing the bull, too! It would probably get two marks.

05 This tries to give two sides. It also has some religious content in it. But how much of it is explained by Dewi – not a lot. He tends to state a series of ideas and reasons, but not give them a lot of explanation. This is true of his style overall. Three out of six marks.

So overall, Dewi got ten out of eighteen marks on this question. If he kept this up all through the paper, he'd probably get a C grade.

Pointers for Stevie's answers on page 33

06 This answer gets full marks as it gives us the process of global warming – even if the English is dodgy!

07 These questions could be answered from one point of view, but you need to explain your ideas in good detail to get full marks for just one side. This answer makes one point which it develops – it is worth two marks. It needs to provide another explained idea to get the full marks.

08 Two ideas is two marks – regardless of it just being a list.

09 This is very vague. No religion is named, and the ideas could come from any one of several. The second half has no religious teachings in it, so isn't worth anything. This would be worth two marks. Use teachings, and apply them to the question to improve this.

10 This gives two sides, and has some religious argument in it. There are a couple of ideas in the first view, and one in the second, but the ideas are developed. It would get four marks. Pushing on from four would need some more ideas on each side and more development.

Overall Stevie got twelve marks from eighteen. If he did this across the whole paper, he'd probably be looking at a B grade.

Pointers for Kerrie's answers on page 47

11 Very good answer, clear and correct, doing exactly what is asked – define and give example. Three marks

12 This gives two sides, one is stronger than the other, but the points made are all valid. There are also some religious arguments in it, so it is worth three marks.

13 When a question about religious attitudes is worth five or six marks, it is best to answer from the point of view of two religions – you simply don't have to work so hard! This answer gives a decent Christian attitude, with application of teachings to the issue of sexism. It also makes a point within the Sikh attitude which is valid in Christianity, so that would help the first part. The Sikh bit is also good, giving two clear beliefs or teachings which are applied. This would get full marks.

14 It is usually not a good idea to bullet point an answer – only do it if you are rapidly running out of time, and need to get a lot of points over. Bullet points don't present as good flowing English, which is what the higher marks require for the exam. They often don't make you explain your ideas very deeply either – again missing those higher marks. This is worth four marks, but rewriting in paragraphs with a bit more depth would probably get it to six.

Overall Kerrie got sixteen marks – carrying on this way would get her an A*.

Pointers for Emma's answers on page 61

16 Three ideas = three marks.

17 This gives two very short points, with no explanation. It can only get two marks.

18 This puts two religions together, but they do make the same points with the same teachings, so that is okay. The answer seems to be applying teachings to the topic of abortion which is good. However, the second half is about why people might agree with abortion – it is irrelevant to this question. That side-track is easy to make, but it eats time, and gets no marks – don't let yourself do it. It is probably worth four marks.

19 This is a one-sided answer, so although it makes a lot of good points and gives lots of religious teachings, it can only get three marks. Make sure you always give two sides in the six-mark questions.

Twelve marks in total; so looking at a B grade if the rest of the paper is of this standard.

Pointers for James' answers on page 75

21 James has passed his answer on the stimulus. This is provided to help you answer the question and here James is able to give a full response referring to some aspects of the work of the UN. You do not however, have to use the example given unless you are told to. Three marks awarded.

22 This is an excellent response. The answer is well focused on the question and the use of the Sikh example supports the reasons he gives. Three marks awarded.

23 Oooops James has made a simple error here – can you see what it is? One mark awarded.

24 James has explained a number of aspects of the Just War theory in Sikhism. Notice that he does not refer to all of the criteria, this isn't necessary as long as the points mentioned are explained as in this example. Four marks awarded.

25 The first part of James response has two good reasons well explained. James also picks up on religious arguments and develops these with reference to beliefs. The alternative side of the argument is not made as well, but does have two relevant reasons. Five marks awarded.

Overall James provides an excellent answer to this question. He scores sixteen out of eighteen and if he maintains this standard in all his responses he is going to achieve an A*.

Pointers for Bethany's answers on page 89

26 Bethany's answer does not make clear that she knows what the generation gap is. She tries to use an example, but needed to develop this to gain the mark. No marks.

27 Bethany refers to several accurate examples here, but has not used them to full effect. A list like this would gain half the marks, but to get full marks she needed to describe in more detail what the events involve and why they are suitable for young people. Two marks awarded.

28 While the examiner might be pleased to hear Bethany has enjoyed her RS lessons, to gain marks she needs to give reasons that support her views. There is only one undeveloped reason in her answer. Can you see it? One mark awarded.

29 Bethany makes similar errors here to those she makes in her answer to part b. She has some good reasons, but states them rather than explains them. The ideas are very specific and there is a little development, so she would achieve three marks.

30 Bethany argues her case quite well using reasons and evidence. She refers to a religious argument and shows awareness of an alternative. This needed to be developed to achieve more than the four marks awarded.

Overall Bethany achieved ten marks and is on her way to a C grade if she scores similar marks in other questions. It is clear that she does have quite a good knowledge and understanding of the subject matter, but has not always tackled the questions well.

Exam bloopers

Even the best candidates can make some silly mistakes on their exam papers and sometimes that one lost mark can be the difference between getting an A* or an A, or a D rather than a C, etc. So here are a few gentle reminders of how to avoid making those costly mistakes.

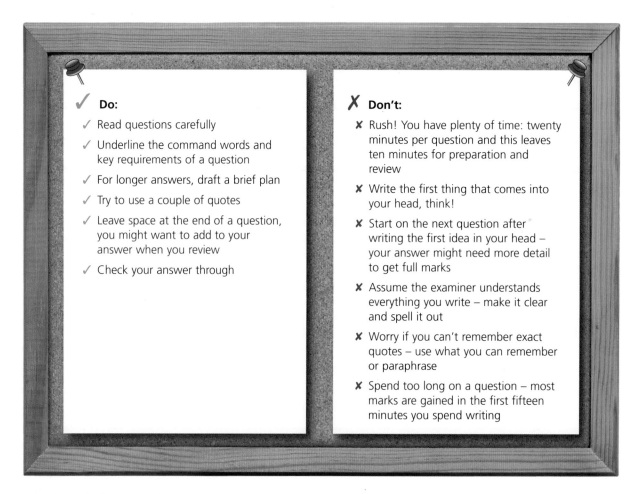

✓ Do:

- ✓ Read questions carefully
- ✓ Underline the command words and key requirements of a question
- ✓ For longer answers, draft a brief plan
- ✓ Try to use a couple of quotes
- ✓ Leave space at the end of a question, you might want to add to your answer when you review
- ✓ Check your answer through

✗ Don't:

- ✗ Rush! You have plenty of time: twenty minutes per question and this leaves ten minutes for preparation and review
- ✗ Write the first thing that comes into your head, think!
- ✗ Start on the next question after writing the first idea in your head – your answer might need more detail to get full marks
- ✗ Assume the examiner understands everything you write – make it clear and spell it out
- ✗ Worry if you can't remember exact quotes – use what you can remember or paraphrase
- ✗ Spend too long on a question – most marks are gained in the first fifteen minutes you spend writing

Exam bloopers – common errors

Some of the common errors candidates make that mean they don't pick up the marks they should have:

- Misreading technical terms and giving wrong definitions as a result.
- Not responding to the correct command word, e.g. writing a detailed description when they were asked to explain.
- Drifting off the question and writing about the issue in general.
- Missing out part of a question.
- Confusing parts of two different questions, so answering parts **a**, **b** and **c** from question 3 then part **d** from question 4 – you've either thrown away a chunk of the marks for three or a chunk for four.
- Running out of time because they write too much for one- and two-mark questions.
- Using bullet points when they need to explain something.
- Not giving examples or religious teachings when they are asked to.
- Not following the rubric (requirements of the exam written on the front of the paper).